Lincoln's Words

Sentiments from the 16th President of the United States

by
Frank C. Brickl

BURD STREET PRESS
SHIPPENSBURG, PENNSYLVANIA

This Burd Street Press publication
was printed by
Beidel Printing House, Inc.
63 West Burd Street
Shippensburg, PA 17257-0708 USA

The acid-free paper used in this book meets the guidelines for
permanence and durability of the Committee on Production Guidelines for Book Longevity of the Council on Library Resources.

For a complete list of available publications
please write
Burd Street Press
Division of White Mane Publishing Company, Inc.
P.O. Box 708
Shippensburg, PA 17257-0708 USA

Library of Congress Cataloging-in-Publication Data

Lincoln, Abraham, 1809-1865.
    Lincoln's words : sentiments from the 16th president of the United States / [compiled]
by Frank C. Brickl.
        p. cm.
    ISBN 1-57249-282-1 (alk. paper)
    1. Lincoln, Abraham, 1809-1865--Quotations. 2. Presidents--United
States--Quotations. 3. United States--Politics and government--1861-1865--Quotations,
maxims, etc. 4. United States--Politics and government--1849-1861--Quotations,
maxims, etc. I. Brickl, Frank C., 1909- II. Title.

E457.99 .L64 2001
973.7'092--dc21

                                                                2001044035

PRINTED IN THE UNITED STATES OF AMERICA

*To
Tiffany, my great-great niece,
and
Alexandra, my great-great-great niece*

Contents

Acknowledgments vii

Introduction ix

Part I. Verbal Portraits 1

Part II. Characterizations 11

Part III. The Prewar Years 25

Part IV. The War Years 35

Acknowledgments

My gal friday, Edith Alt, for her patience in deciphering and typing my handwritten manuscript.

My great-great niece, Karen Weiss Gust, for her interest.

Tom Fargen, Jr., for loaning me his books about Lincoln.

Viola Tank, a neighbor, for loaning me a pamphlet about Lincoln.

The personnel of the Sauk City Library for their willingness to help.

Introduction

In 1979 a friend loaned me a copy of Carl Sandburg's *Abraham Lincoln: The Prairie Years and the War Years*. Shortly after I started reading it I found out that my friend was being transferred out of state. In order to return the copy before she left, I read the book as fast as I could—having many other obligations to tend to at the same time. In this experience of speed reading I found that, as good as Sandburg's writing was, the only parts that really interested me were Lincoln's quotations.

Fifteen years later now, being retired, I figured that perhaps there are others who feel as I did—being interested more in Lincoln himself than in any other persons or events surrounding him. Therefore, I leisurely reread Sandburg's *Abraham Lincoln*, while at the same time I noted all direct quotations of the man.

I also read other books about Lincoln including *With Malice Toward None: The Life of Abraham Lincoln* by Stephen B. Oates. I noted quotations from this book too.

Of course, I read many books about the Civil War—not only its formal battles but of how the war affected lives "at home." Possibly the most interesting of these was *Mary Chesnut's Civil War.*

The best book I read on the subject of the rebellion was Bruce Catton's *Civil War,* mostly a detailed account of strategy and battle. There may be a quotation or two derived from this work.

I have included in part four of this book the Second Emancipation Proclamation, the Gettysburg Address, and the Second Inaugural Address. These three documents, to me, reflect the soul of Lincoln. If voting were still a process in declaring a person a saint, I, as a Catholic priest, would vote "aye" for Abraham Lincoln.

BRICKBATS	BOUQUETS
lacked executive ability	a joker
a beast	unique
unmethodical	plain working man
an honest ape	unspotted character
a monster	chief joker
an idiot	sober
no culture	grim
an abortion	solemn
no education	a jewel
too slow	tormented
too hesitant	awkward humors
love of power	delicate
charlatan	tenuous
inordinate vanity	perfectly lonely
consummate dissembler	lonely
sagacious demagogue	faithful
cunning	consecrated
writhing	shrewd peasant
elusive	noble

BRICKBATS *(contd.)*   BOUQUETS *(contd.)*

repugnant   chain breaker (slavery)

damnable   railsplitter

puerile   stern

harmless   inflexible

unscrupulous knave   bold

fanatic   vigilant

mean   sleepless energy

                               untiring

                               genius

Verbal Portraits

Rev. Gariy Wankerl

A coal heaver: "Abe, they say you're the tallest man in the United States, but I don't believe you are taller than I am." President-elect Lincoln: "Come up here and let's measure." Back to back they were the same height—6 feet, 4 inches.

* * *

On July 9, 1862, Chaplain Joseph Twichell wrote the following description of Lincoln reviewing the troops of the Army of the Potomac:

> It did seem as though the President's legs would become entangled with those of the horse he rode and both come down together...That arm with which he drew the rein, in its angles and position resembled the hind legs of a grasshopper— the hand before—the elbow away back over the horse's tail. The removal of his hat before each regiment was also a source of laughter in the style of its execution—the quick trot of the horse making it a feat of some difficulty, while from the same cause, his hold on it, while off, seemed very precarious. But, the boys

liked him, in fact his popularity with the army is and has been unsurpassed. Most of our rulers and leaders fall into odium, but all have faith in Lincoln.

* * *

Walt Whitman wrote to the *New York Times* in the summer of 1863:

I see the President almost every day...as he passes to or from his lodgings out of town...Mr. Lincoln generally rides a good-sized easy-going gray horse, is dressed in plain black, somewhat rusty and dusty; wears a black stiff hat, and looks about as ordinary in attire, and, as the commonest man...I saw very plainly the President's dark brown face, with deep cut lines, the eyes, etc., always to me with a deep latent sadness in the expression...None of the artists have caught the deep, though subtle and indirect, expression of this man's face. They have only caught the surface. There is something else there. One of the great portrait painters of two or three centuries ago is needed.

* * *

In a letter to two boys in New York, Walt Whitman wrote it March 1863:

> I think well of the President. He has a face like a Hoosier Michelangelo, so awful ugly it becomes beautiful, with its strong mouth, its deep cut, crisscross lines, and its doughnut complexion...He has shown, I sometimes think, an almost supernatural tact in keeping the ship afloat at all.

* * *

George Templeton Strong, a New York lawyer, wrote of Lincoln in his diary:

> He's a barbarian, Scythian, yahoo, a gorilla, in respect of outward polish, but a most sensible, straightforward old codger. The best president we have had since old Jackson's time.

* * *

Edward Dicey, an English author, stated that Lincoln's stories "read dull enough in print, unless you could give also the dry chuckle with which they were accompanied, and the gleam in the speaker's eye, as, with the action habitual to him, he rubs his hand down the side of his long leg."

* * *

John Nicolay, one of Lincoln's secretaries: "Graphic art was powerless before a face that moved through a thousand delicate gradations of line and contour, light and shade, sparkle of the eye and curve of the lip, in the long gamut of expression from grave to gay, and back again from the rollicking jollity of laughter to that far-away look."

* * *

"Something about the man, the face, is unfathomable." Gustave Koerner.

* * *

Congressman Henry Laurens Dawes of Massachusetts, early in the administration, said: "There is something in his face I cannot understand...(it is) a title page of anxiety and distress."

* * *

"Lincoln is letting his whiskers grow now," men were saying in January (1861) when his upper lip and cheeks were shaved but a stubble left on the chin. Then in February hair had grown over jaws, chin and throat, the upper lip shaven. This facial design was wrought by William Florville, a Haitian-born colored man, known as Billy the Barber, whose shop in Springfield, Illinois dated back to 1831. In the house of this barber, the first Catholic mass is said to have been offered in Springfield.

* * *

"What do you know 'bout Massa Linkum? Massa Linkum be everywhere. He walk de earth like de Lord." A white-headed Negro.

* * *

The President rises slowly, draws from his pocket a paper, and, when commotion subsides, in a sharp, unmusical treble voice, reads the brief and pithy remarks.

A reporter wrote about the Gettysburg Address.

* * *

By the time we had reached the troops he was completely covered with dust, and the black color of his clothes had changed to Confederate gray...his trousers gradually worked up above his ankles, and gave him the appearance of a country farmer riding into town wearing his Sunday clothes. However, the troops were so lost in admiration of the man that the humorous aspect did not seem to strike them. The soldiers rapidly passed the word along the line that "Uncle Abe" had joined them, and cheers broke forth from all the commands, and enthusiastic shouts and even words of familiar greeting met him on all sides.

Horace Porter reporting Lincoln's and son Tad's visit to the Army of the Potomac—June 21, 1864.

* * *

At the 18th Corps camp Lincoln met a torrent of black men who circled round about him. Tears ran down some faces. Cheers, laughter, songs, mixed and rang in the air. "God bress Massa Linkum!" "De

Lawd save Fader Abraham!" They waved their arms, kissed the hands of their mystic hero, crowded around fondling his horse, bridle and saddle. The President rode with bared head; the tears had started to his eyes and his voice was broken.

Horace Porter on Lincoln's visit to the army—June 21, 1864.

* * *

"I think Jefferson (Davis) will succeed." "Why does thee think so?" "Because Jefferson is a praying man." "And so is Abraham a praying man." "Yes, but the Lord will think Abraham is joking." Two Quakeresses in a railway coach.

Characterizations

The things I want to know are in books; my best friend is the man who'll git me a book I ain't read. An early observation.

* * *

Who has the most right to complain, the Indian or the Negro? An early question.

* * *

Ya never cuss a good axe. After nearly cutting off his thumb.

* * *

Who makes state lines? What are state lines? An observation.

* * *

There's a school and thousands of books there and fellers that know everything in creation. On New Harmony, Indiana, on the Wabash River.

* * *

Let auld acquaintance be forgot
And never brought to mind;

May Jackson be our President
And Adams left behind.

Lincolnesque ditty.

* * *

Now sunburnt till it was a combine of colors! His own black hat.

* * *

Oh, I guess I can make a few rabbit tracks. When asked whether he could write.

* * *

I'll fight you, John, if you'll chalk your size on me. And every blow outside counts foul. When challenged to fight by a small man.

* * *

The corn is getting high, isn't it? To Ann Rutledge.

* * *

It can't happen that a sucker like me could have a gal like her. About Ann Rutledge.

* * *

Bring on your man from Sand Ridge. I can do him up in three shakes of a sheep's tail, and I can whip the whole pack of you if you give me ten minutes between fights. To a group goading for a fight.

* * *

If the good people in their wisdom shall see fit to keep me in the background, I have been too familiar with disappointments to be very much chagrined. First run for Illinois legislature.

* * *

That reminds me of a feller down in Indiany. Introduction to a story.

* * *

My politics are short and sweet, like the old woman's dance...If elected I shall be thankful; if not it will be all the same.

* * *

Dogskin gloves? I'll tell you how I know. Jack Clary's dog killed Tom Wadkins' sheep and

Tom Wadkins' boy killed the dog, old John Mounts tanned the dogskin and Sally Spears made the gloves. That's the way I know they're dogskin.

* * *

Time, what an empty vapor 'tis. From his early verse.

* * *

By Jing! Lincoln's profanity.

* * *

I am decidedly opposed to the people's money being used to pay the fiddler.

* * *

Some will prefer opulent knavery to honest poverty. To the legislature.

* * *

In a government like ours, public sentiment is everything, determining what laws and decisions can and cannot be enforced.

* * *

I found the calves all together and away from the cows, and I didn't know my calf well enough to distinguish her from the others. Still, I picked out one that I thought was mine. Presently that identical calf went and sucked my cow, and then I knew it was mine. On getting his cow to be milked.

* * *

There are few things wholly evil or wholly good. A Lincoln motto.

* * *

This rain makes the corn laugh. After a needed rain.

* * *

You'll have to get some other fellow to win this case for you. I couldn't do it. All the while I'd be talking to that jury I'd be thinking "Lincoln, you're a liar," and I believe I should forget myself and say it out loud. On rejecting a client.

* * *

Being elected to Congress, though I am very grateful to our friends for having done it, has not pleased me as much as I expected. On being elected.

* * *

To secure to each laborer the whole product of his labor, or as nearly as possible, is a worthy object of any government on economics. Before going to Washington as a representative in 1847.

* * *

...military glory—that attractive rainbow that rises in showers of blood—that serpent's eye that charms to destroy—...How like the half-insane mumbling of a fever dream is the whole war part of his late message! On President James K. Polk's message on the war with Mexico.

* * *

He knows not where he is. He is a bewildered, confounded, and miserably perplexed man. About Polk and the war with Mexico.

* * *

An honest laborer digs coal at about seventy cents a day, while the President digs abstractions at about seventy dollars a day. The coal is clearly worth more than the abstractions. From a speech to Congress, 1848.

* * *

To pay for canals with canal tolls and tonnage duties, before canals were dug, was like the Irishman and his new boots. "I shall never git 'em on till I wear 'em a day or two, and stretch 'em a little." To Congress, 1848.

* * *

Excuse this short letter. I have so many to write that I cannot devote much time to any one. Yours as ever. To Archibald Williams, 1848.

* * *

Your letter is exceedingly painful to me; and I cannot but think there is some mistake in your impression of the motives of the old men. To his friend and partner William H. Herndon in Illinois.

* * *

The thing that struck me most forcibly when I saw the Falls was, where in the world all the water came from. Asked what impressed him most about Niagara Falls.

* * *

In the Mexican War the United States was like the farmer, who said: "I ain't greedy; I only want what jines mine!" Stumping Illinois in 1848.

* * *

If the Church would ask simply for assent to the Savior's statement of the substance of the law: "Thou shalt love the Lord thy God with all thy heart, and with all thy soul, and with all thy mind, and thy neighbor as thyself"; that church would I gladly unite with. To Mrs. Rankin on religion.

* * *

She trusted in Providence till the britchin' broke, and then she didn't know "what on airth to do." About a woman whose horse ran away with her in the buggy.

* * *

She'll be down as soon as she gets her trotting harness on. To two women who came to visit Mrs. Lincoln.

* * *

What did Mrs. Lincoln say? was Lincoln's question. *"She said yes." Then in God's name, cut it down to the roots.* When asked about cutting down a tree on the Lincoln property.

* * *

I am afraid you will get so well and fat and young as to be wanting to marry again. To Mary on her gaining weight and health.

* * *

Jim, you'll have to lift your loft a little higher; I can't straighten out under it very well. When getting milk from the neighbor when his own cow was dry.

* * *

Little people require less wood and wool to keep them comfortable. To a short neighbor woman.

* * *

Although volume upon volume is written to prove slavery a good thing, we never hear of the man who wishes to take the good of it by being a slave himself. Lincoln's indictment of slavery.

* * *

I am not a temperance man, but I am temperate to this extent: I don't drink. During the temperance movement in Illinois.

* * *

Nix com raus. In his letters while studying German.

* * *

I am never easy when I am handling a thought, till I have bounded it north, bounded it south, bounded it east, and bounded it west. About himself.

* * *

In this troublesome world we are never quite satisfied. A remark.

* * *

The ant who has toiled and dragged a crumb to his nest will furiously defend the fruit of his labor against whatever robber assails him. On slavery.

* * *

I shall never be glad again. In assessing the country's problems.

* * *

The Lord prefers common looking people. That is the reason He makes so many of them. On the Lord and the common man.

* * *

I never behold them (the heavens filled with stars) that I do not feel I am looking in the face of God. I can see how it might be possible for a man to look down upon the earth and be an atheist, but I cannot conceive how he could look up into the heavens and say there is no God. On the heavens.

* * *

In regard to this great Book, I have but to say, it is the best gift God has given to men. All the good Savior gave to the world was communicated through this Book. But without it, we could not know right from wrong. All things most desirable for men's welfare, here and hereafter, are to be found portrayed in it. On the Bible.

The Prewar Years

It's been my experience that folks who have no vices have very few virtues. Quoting a Kentuckian.

* * *

I feel like the little boy who stumped his toe; I'm too big to cry and too badly burnt to laugh. After losing to Stephen Douglas.

* * *

We are not going to let the Republican Party become a mere sucked egg, all shell and no meat—the principle all sucked out. About accepting Popular Sovereignty for the states.

* * *

I hain't been caught lyin' yet and I don't mean to be. To a lawyer.

* * *

A man has no time to spend half his life in quarrels. On an opponent's defeat.

* * *

So you are the little lady who started this big war? Greeting Harriet Beecher Stowe during the Civil War.

* * *

A funny story...of genuine wit, has the same effect on me that I suppose a good square drink of whiskey has on a toper, it puts new life into me. An observation.

* * *

When men wrangle by the mouth with no certainty that they mean the same thing while using the same words, it perhaps would be as well if they would keep silent. On his journey to the first inaugural.

* * *

I esteem them no better than other people, nor any worse. On Germans and other foreigners.

* * *

She wrote me that I would be better looking if I wore whiskers. You see I let these whiskers grow for you, Grace. In New York to Grace Bedell, a little girl.

* * *

Jim used to say that his brother was the damndest scoundrel that ever lived, but in the infinite mercy of Providence he was also the damndest fool. To friends.

* * *

I have the best of the bargain in the sight. To some ladies on his first inaugural route.

* * *

I have neither the voice nor the strength to address you. When informed that Jefferson Davis took the oath of office as president of six Confederacy states, February 18, 1861, in Montgomery, Alabama.

* * *

Question: *Are we really to have civil war?* Lincoln's answer: *When I was a young lawyer, and Illinois was little settled, I, with other lawyers, used to ride the circuit. Once a long*

*spell of pouring rain flooded the whole coun-
try. Ahead of us was Fox River, larger than all
the rest, and we could not help saying to each
other, "If these small streams give us so much
trouble, how shall we get over the Fox River?"
Darkness fell before we had reached that
stream, and we all stopped at a log tavern,
had our horses put up and resolved to spend
the night. Here we were right glad to fall in
with the Methodist Presiding Elder of the circuit, who rode it in all weather, knew all its
ways, and could tell us all about Fox River. So
we all gathered around him and asked him if
he knew about the crossing of Fox River. "Oh
yes," he replied. "I know all about Fox River. I
have crossed it often and understand it well.
But I have one fixed rule with regard to Fox
River: I never cross it till I reach it."*

* * *

*If it (the Ship of State) should suffer at-
tack now, there will be no pilot ever needed
for another voyage.* In New York, on his way
to the inauguration.

* * *

If this country cannot be saved without giving up that principle—(i.e., the Declaration of Independence), I was about to say I would rather be assassinated on this spot than to surrender it. In Philadelphia, February 23, 1861.

* * *

What would the nation think of its President stealing into its Capitol like a thief in the night? In response to plans to enter Washington secretly to avoid the assassination plot against the president in Baltimore.

* * *

How can I justify my title of Honest Ole Abe with the appointment of a man like Cameron? On finally appointing Simon Cameron as secretary of war.

* * *

No! No! I won't open shop in the street. When handed a job request at an intersection.

* * *

If our American society and the United States government are demoralized and overthrown, it will come from the voracious desire for of-fice, this wriggle to live without toil, work and labor, from which I am not free myself. On pa-tronage seekers.

* * *

This man wants to work—so uncommon a want that I think it ought to be gratified. To a department head.

* * *

The lady bearer of this says she has two sons who want to work. Set them at it if pos-sible. Wanting to work is so rare a want that it should be encouraged. To a department head.

* * *

Yes, and it's a pretty mess you got me into. To a job seeker who reminded Lincoln that he helped to elect him.

* * *

God help me! It is said I offended you. Please tell me how. To Senator Jacob Collamer of Vermont.

* * *

Oh well, I guess we'll manage to keep house. When warned by William Tecumseh Sherman that they were preparing for war in Louisiana—mid-March 1861.

* * *

(There are) ten pegs where there is but one hole to put them in. About job seekers.

* * *

Well sir, I am glad to know that you have not come after an office. To a visitor.

* * *

I will endeavor to apply the rule of give and take. To New York politicians on patronage.

* * *

This will raise distinctly the question of union or disunion. To Secretary of State William H. Seward, on Fort Sumter.

* * *

...I remark that if this must be done, I must do it. To Seward's wild proposal for war with Spain and France.

* * *

I am like a man so busy letting rooms in one end of his house, that I can't stop to put out the fire that is burning in the other. To Henry J. Raymond of the *Times* in the first month of his presidency.

The War Years

What have I done wrong? As war was coming closer.

* * *

I think the necessity for being ready increases. Look to it. To Governor Andrew G. Curtin of Pennsylvania, April 10, 1861.

* * *

<u>April 12, 1861 Confederate Navy bombarded Fort Sumter; the Civil War begins.</u>

On April 14, Fort Sumter was evacuated with one casualty.

* * *

Now therefore, I, Abraham Lincoln, President of the United States, in virtue of the power in me vested by the Constitution and the laws, have thought fit to call forth, the militia of the several States of the Union to the aggregate number of seventy-five thousand, in order to suppress said combinations, and to cause the laws to be duly executed. In response to the secessionist states: South Carolina, Georgia,

Alabama, Florida, Mississippi, Louisiana, and Texas, April 14, 1861.

* * *

In every event, the utmost care will be observed, consistently with the objects aforesaid, to avoid any devastation, any destruction of, or interference with property, or any disturbance of peaceful citizens. To the Volunteer Navy, April 14, 1861.

* * *

My policy is to have no policy. To his secretary John Hay in April 1861. (*I'll fight secession leaders til hell is froze over and then fight on the ice.* Parson Brownlow in Knoxville, Tennessee.)

* * *

For my own part, I consider the first necessity that is upon us, is of proving that popular government is not an absurdity. We must settle this question now—whether in a free government the minority have the right to break it up whenever they choose. To John Hay in the first week of the rebellion.

* * *

This has been my flag and shall be till the end...for a thousand years and afterward as long as heaven permits, without limit of duration. Archbishop John Hughes of New York in a letter for public reading.

* * *

It became necessary for me to choose whether I should let the government fall at once into ruin, or whether...I would make an effort to save it. On assuming presidential war powers.

* * *

I suppose there is room enough to bury 75,000 in her soil. When told that 75,000 Marylanders would oppose the passage of troops over her soil.

* * *

You have all heard of the Irishman who, when a fellow was cutting his throat with a blunt razor, complained that he haggled it. Now, if I can't have troops direct through Maryland, and must have them all the way around by water, or marched across out-of-the-way territory, I shall be haggled. To delegates from Baltimore about troops crossing Maryland.

* * *

Others have been made fools of by the girls; but this can never with truth be said of me. I most emphatically, in this instance, made a fool of myself. On being jilted.

* * *

The large sums foolishly, not to say completely thrown away, constitute one of the just causes of complaint against the administration. To the legislature.

* * *

Broken by it, I too may be, bow to it I never will. On corruption.

* * *

No woman ever went astray without a man to help her. From a Lincoln rhyme.

* * *

I am now the most miserable man living. If what I feel were equally distributed to the whole human family, there would not be one cheerful face on the earth. After breaking up with Mary Todd.

* * *

If I were you, in case my mind were not exactly right, I would avoid being idle. To his friend Speed.

* * *

You shall no more be able to pierce him than to penetrate the hard shell of a tortoise with a rye straw. On distributing reform.

* * *

The practice of drinking is just as old as the world itself. On alcohol.

* * *

Even then it was known and acknowledged that many were greatly injured by it. I.e., alcoholic drink.

* * *

The victims of it were to be pitied and compassionated, just as are the heirs of consumption and other hereditary diseases. On excessive drinkers.

* * *

Better lay down the spade you are stealing, Paddy; if you don't you'll pay for it at the day of judgment. On stopping drinking.

* * *

Deceit and falsehood, especially if you have got a bad memory, is the worst enemy a fellow can have. To a cadet.

* * *

One drop of honey catches more flies than a half gallon of gall: Load your musket with this maxim, and smoke it in your pipe. To same cadet.

* * *

If you make a bad bargain, hug it all the tighter. On marriage.

* * *

I am so poor and make so little headway in the world, that I drop back in a month of idleness as much as I gain in a year's sowing. 1841.

* * *

How about cow dung at five paces? On weapons for a duel.

* * *

I am going to be married today. To a friend, November 4, 1842.

* * *

With this ring (inscribed, "Love is eternal.") I thee endow with all my goods, chattels, lands and tenements. Marriage to Mary Todd, November 4, 1842.

* * *

Nothing is new here, except my marrying which, to me, is a matter of profound wonder. To a friend five days after marriage.

* * *

Every man must skin his own skunk. One of his father's proverbs.

* * *

...cats wailing with pain and spitting at each other at night outside the hotel rooms. In the morning perhaps the alley would be full of dead cats—so the sounds indicated. But in the morning the cats were at peace, with assured futures. On squabbling politicians.

* * *

Why don't they come! Why don't they come! Looking out a White House window expecting volunteers for the war.

* * *

I don't believe there is any North! The Seventh Regiment is a myth! Rhode Island is not known in our geography any longer! You are the Northern realities. To a few Massachusetts wounded coming through Baltimore, April 24, 1861.

* * *

Excuse me, but I cannot talk... Weeping after Colonel Ephraim E. Ellsworth was shot after removing the Confederate flag from the Marshall House hotel in Alexandria, Virginia, May 24, 1861.

* * *

In the untimely loss of your noble son, our affliction here, is scarcely less than your own...May God give you that consolation which is beyond all earthly power. To Colonel Ellsworth's parents.

* * *

You are green, it is true, but they are green also. To a hesitant General Irvin McDowell before the Battle of Bull Run, July 21, 1861.

* * *

Union losses in the Battle of Bull Run: 16 officers and 444 men killed; 78 officers and 1,046 men wounded; and 50 officers and 1,262 men missing. Confederate losses: 378 killed, 1,489 wounded, and 30 missing.

* * *

Well boys, I have a great deal of respect for Colonel Sherman, and if he turned you out of the barn, I have no doubt it was for some good purpose. I presume he thought you would feel better if you went to work and tried to forget your troubles. To soldiers who complained about being evicted from a barn to make room for horses.

* * *

Well, if I were you, and he threatened to shoot, I would not trust him, for I believe he would do it. To an officer who told Lincoln that Sherman threatened to shoot him.

* * *

I don't care a cornhusk for those who think that a statesman, like a blind horse in a tread-mill, needs no rest or that, like the conventional whitewashed statue of justice, he must always pose for dignified effect. Before taking a short holiday (vacation).

* * *

I will hold McClellan's horse if he will only bring us success. In response to complaints about General George B. McClellan.

* * *

You are quite a female politician. To Jesse Frémont, wife of General John C. Frémont.

* * *

Oh, that'll be got along with. When asked about the problem of imminent war with England.

* * *

Your question reminds me of an incident which occurred out West. Two roughs were playing cards for high stakes, when one of them, suspecting his adversary of foul play, straightway drew his bowie knife from his belt and pinned the hand of the other player upon the table, exclaiming, "If you haven't got the ace of spades under your palm, I'll apologize." In answer to a question: "Is it to be war or peace?" (With England)

* * *

There will be no war unless England is bent on having one. To Charles Sumner.

* * *

One war at a time. To William H. Seward, on possibility of war with England.

* * *

The English didn't give us time to turn around. It was very humiliating but we had one big war on hand and we didn't want two at the same time. On refusing two prisoners from the English ship *Trenton*—as demanded by the English.

* * *

It was a pretty bitter pill to swallow, but I contented myself with believing that England's triumph in the matter would be short-lived and that after ending our war successfully we would be so powerful that we could call her to account for all the embarrassments she had inflicted on us. I felt a good deal like the sick man in Illinois who was told he probably hadn't many days longer to live and that he ought to make peace with any enemies he might have. He said that the man he hated worst of all was a fellow named Brown in the next village and he guessed he had better begin on him. So Brown was sent for, and when he came, the sick man began to say, in a voice "as weak as Moses" that he wanted to die at peace with all his fellow creatures, and he hoped that he and Brown could now shake hands and bury all their enmity. The scene was becoming all too pathetic for Brown, who had got out his handkerchief and wiped the gathering tears from his eyes. It wasn't long before he melted and gave his hand to his neighbor, and they had a regular love-feast. After a parting that would have softened the heart of a grindstone, Brown had about reached the room door, when the sick man rose up on his elbow and said, "But see here, Brown, if I should happen to get well, mind that old grudge stands." On giving in to England's demands.

* * *

There are already among us those, who, if the Union be preserved, will live to see it contain 250 millions. The struggle of today, is not altogether for today—it is for a vast future also. Message to Congress, 1861.

* * *

...now therefore, be it known, that I, Abraham Lincoln, President of the United States of America, have granted and do hereby grant unto him, the said Nathaniel Gordon, a respite of the above recited sentence, until Friday, the 21st day of February, A.D. 1862, between the hours of twelve o'clock at noon and three o'clock in the afternoon of the said day, when the said sentence shall be executed. In granting this respite it becomes my painful duty to admonish the prisoner that, relinquishing all expectation of pardon by Human Authority, he refer himself alone to the energy of the common God and Father of

all men. On refusing to pardon a convicted slave trader.

* * *

Wade, ANYBODY will do for you, but I must have SOMEBODY. When asked by Benjamin Franklin Wade to replace General McClellan with anybody.

* * *

Yes, that's a fact. I see the point now, but I don't know anything about the Law of Nations and I thought it was alright. When reminded by Congressman Thaddeus Stevens that in declaring a blockade of the seceded states he was tacitly acknowledging Southern independence.

* * *

Early in Lincoln's administration, Congressman Thaddeus Stevens warned the president that Simon Cameron had taking ways and might not be the man to head the War Department. *You don't mean to say that Cameron would steal?* Lincoln asked. *No*, was the reply. *I don't think he would steal a red hot stove.* Lincoln repeated this to Cameron considering it a criticism and a warning to the secretary of war. Cameron did not consider it funny and insisted that Stevens retract. So Stevens, visiting at the White House, asked, *Mr. Lincoln, why did you tell Cameron what I said to you?* Lincoln answered, *I thought it was a good joke and didn't think it would make him mad. Well,* Stevens replied. *He is very mad and made me promise to retract. I will now do so. I believe I told you he would not steal a red hot stove. I now take that back.*

* * *

Gentlemen, if you want Secretary Cameron removed, you have only to bring me one proved case of dishonesty and I promise you his head! But I assure you that I am not going to act on what seems to me the most unfounded gossip. To a group demanding the removal of Simon Cameron as secretary of war because of the many abuses in war contracts.

* * *

It is a good thing for individuals that there is a government to shove their acts upon. No man's shoulders are broad enough to bear what must be. To his secretary John G. Nicolay about the many accusations of abuses, thievery and dishonesty in all aspects of the war effort.

* * *

This will never do, General Cameron must take no such responsibility. That is a question which belongs exclusively to me. On Secretary of War Cameron's directive to confiscate and arm rebel slaves.

* * *

As you have more than once expressed a desire for a change of position, I can now gratify you, consistently with my view of public interest. I therefore propose nominating you to the Senate, next Monday, as minister to Russia. To Simon Cameron, January 11, 1862.

* * *

We may have to treat him as they are sometimes obliged to treat a Methodist minister I know out West. He gets wrought up to so high a pitch of excitement in his prayers and ex-hortations, that they are obliged to put bricks in his pockets to keep him down. We may be obliged to serve Stanton in the same way, but I guess we'll let him jump a while first. In re-ply to complaints about Edwin McMasters Stanton, the newly appointed secretary of war, after Cameron's release.

* * *

I suppose you have good reasons for it; and having good reasons, I am glad. I knew nothing about it until it was done. To Secre-tary of War Stanton who had General Charles P. Stone arrested in the Ball's Bluff disaster.

* * *

It is due to Mr. Cameron to say that, al-though he fully approved the proceedings, they were not moved nor suggested by himself, and that not only the President but all other heads of departments were at least equally respon-sible with him for whatever error, wrong, or fault was committed in the premises. In response to

Congress's attempt to censure Simon Cameron after his release from office.

* * *

Why in hell and damnation ain't they ready? To a staff officer who informed Lincoln that General McClellan's army was unable to move because the pontoon bridges were not ready.

* * *

I had (have) just obtained from the Secretary of War, a statement, taken as he said, from your own returns, making 108,000 then with you and enroute to you. You now say you will have but 85,000 when all enroute to you shall have reached you. How can the discrepancy of 23,000 be accounted for? Once more let me tell you, it is indispensible to you that you strike a blow, I am powerless to help him. To McClellan who constantly requested more men and supplies but decided not to engage in battle.

* * *

It has pleased Almighty God to vouchsafe signal victories to the land and naval forces engaged in suppressing an internal rebellion, and at the same time to avert from our country the dangers of foreign intervention and invasion. From Lincoln's proclamation after the victory at Shiloh, which was won under General Ulysses S. Grant in Tennessee.

* * *

I can't spare this man—he fights. In response to requests that General Grant be dismissed for drunkenness after the Battle of Shiloh.

* * *

The doll Jack is pardoned. By order of the President A. Lincoln. To his boys Tad and Willie who condemned their doll soldier for sleeping on picket duty.

* * *

It is hard, hard, hard to have him die. After son Willie's death.

* * *

All I have to say is what the girl said when she put her foot into the stocking. It strikes me there's something in it. Lincoln's response on holding a pasteboard model of Ericsson's *Monitor*, the small metal battleship that revolutionized battleship construction.

* * *

Oh, that is Stanton's navy...as useless as the paps of a man to a sucking child. They may be some show to amuse the child, but they are good for nothing for service. On inspecting a long line of wooden navy boats near Kettle Bottom Schools on the Potomac River.

* * *

It is not so. It is you who honor me and your country, and I will promote you. After Lieutenant John Worden said to the visiting Lincoln, *You do me great honor.*

* * *

He (McClellan) seemed to think, in defiance of Scripture, that heaven sent its rain only on the just and not on the unjust. To his secretary

John Hay on General McClellan's constant complaint about the rain and mud, which kept him from going on the attack.

* * *

My son, I think your country can afford to get you a new pair of breeches. To a boyish-looking lieutenant who failed to get a new issue of clothing after a week of battles and retreats in mud and rain.

* * *

He's got the slows. On General McClellan's inability and/or refusal to move the army.

* * *

I expect to maintain this contest until successful, or till I die, or am conquered, or my term expires, or Congress or the country forsakes me. In a letter making his position clear.

* * *

I was as nearly inconsolable as I could be and live. After General McClellan's retreat from Malvern Hill, 20 miles from Richmond.

* * *

Sending men to that army is like shoveling fleas across a barnyard—not half of them get there. If I gave McClellan all the men he asks for, they could not find room to lie down. They'd have to sleep standing up. On General McClellan's repeated demands for more men and supplies.

* * *

Gen'l, I understand you have used the word "capitulate"—that is a word not to be used in connection with our army... To R. B. Marcy, McClellan's chief of staff and father-in-law.

* * *

If by magic he (General in Chief Halleck) could reinforce McClellan with 100,000 men today, he would be in ecstasy over it, thank him for it and tell him that he would go to Richmond tomorrow, but when tomorrow came he would telegraph that he had certain information that the enemy had 400,000 men, and that he could not advance without reinforcements. To Senator Orville H. Browning.

* * *

Browning, I must die sometime. When the senator expressed concern about Lincoln's health, worries, and stress.

* * *

Go home and read Proverbs 30:10. To a man who complained about a superior officer.

* * *

A story. Lincoln demanded more detailed reports from McClellan, so the general telegraphed: *Have captured two cows. What disposition should I make of them?* Lincoln's reply: *Milk 'em, George.*

* * *

Well, how does it look today? After a complete reorganization of the war effort in late 1862.

* * *

A coffee mill gun. On inspecting a model of a machine gun operated with a crank.

* * *

That can't hurt you with us. To a Prussian prince fighting for the Union.

* * *

Have you heard the Rebel song, "Dixie"? To a French count, his guest on the *River Queen. The tune is now Federal property, and it's good to show the Rebels that with us in power, they will be free to hear it again. It has always been a favorite of mine, and since we've captured it, we have a perfect right to enjoy it.* And Lincoln, in the last week of his life, asked the band to play it.

* * *

Please say to these gentlemen that if they do not work quickly I will make quick work with them. In the name of all that is reasonable, how long does it take to pay a couple of Regiments? When paymasters caused a delay in transporting troops.

* * *

Rt. Rev. Sir: I am sure you will pardon me if, in my ignorance, I do not address (you) with technical correctness...If you perceive no objection, I will thank you to give me the name or names of one or more suitable persons of the Catholic Church, to whom I may with propriety, tender the same service. To Archbishop John Hughes on the appointment of Catholic chaplains, after having appointed three Protestant chaplains.

* * *

Many thanks for your kind and judicious letters to Gov. Seward, and which he regularly allows me both the pleasure and the profit of perusing. To Archbishop John Hughes, an outspoken Unionist.

* * *

If in such a difficulty as this you do not help, you fail me precisely in the point for which I sought your assistance. To General in Chief Henry W. Halleck who failed to direct and failed also to investigate the many failures and defeats of the Army of the Potomac.

* * *

Get a good ready and start on Monday. To General McDowell who objected to start a battle on Sunday.

* * *

Not very graceful. But I'm growing old enough not to care much for the manner of doing things. To John Hay, his secretary.

* * *

Well John, we are whipped again, I am afraid. The enemy reinforced on Pope and drove back his left wing and he has retired to Centerville where he says he will be able to hold his men. I don't like that expression. I don't like to hear him admit his men need holding. To John Hay upon hearing of Major General John Pope's retreat on August 20, 1862.

* * *

Chase says we can't raise any more money; Pope is licked and McClellan has the diarrhea. What shall I do? The bottom is out of the tub, the bottom is out of the tub. To

John Hay after John Pope's defeat at the second Battle of Bull Run.

* * *

That man Haupt has built a bridge across Potomac Creek, about 400 feet long and nearly 100 feet high over which loaded trains are running every hour, and upon my word, gentlemen, there is nothing in it but beanpoles and cornstalks. About Colonel Herman Haupt under whose command railroads kept the Union armies supplied.

* * *

We had the enemy in the hollow of our hands on Friday, if our generals, who are vexed with Pope, had done their duty; all of our present difficulties and reverses have been brought upon us by these quarrels of the generals. To Secretary of the Navy Gideon Welles after Pope's dismissal.

* * *

(I am) reminded of a revival meeting in Illinois when a fellow with a few drinks too

many in him had walked up the aisle to a front pew. All eyes were on him, but he didn't care; he joined in the singing, droned amen at the close of prayers, and as the meeting proceeded, dozed off in sleep. Before the meeting ended, the pastor asked the usual question: "Who are on the Lord's side?" and the congregation arose en masse. When the pastor asked, "Who are on the side of the Devil?" the dozing sleeper came to, heard part of the question, saw the parson standing, arose to his feet to say: "I don't exactly understand the question but I'll stand by you, parson, to the last. But it seems to me," he added reflectively, "that we're in a hopeless minority." After a cabinet meeting where all but one member were against the president.

* * *

He (McClellan) has acted badly in this matter, but we must use what tools we have. There is no man in the army who can man these fortifications and lick these troops into shape half as well as he. Unquestionably he has acted badly toward Pope. He wanted him to fail. That is unpardonable. But he is too useful just now to sacrifice. If he can't fight himself, he excels in making others ready to fight...and calling him (McClellan) to power again was a great deal like curing the bite with the hair of a dog. On returning George B. McClellan to again lead the Army of the Potomac.

* * *

I think we'd better wait; perhaps a real fighting general will come along some of these days, and then we'll all be happy. If you go to mixing in a mix-up, you only make the muddle worse. On advice to again change generals.

* * *

God bless you, and all with you. Destroy the rebel army, if possible. To General McClellan before the Battle of Antietam.

* * *

Whatever the troops and people may think and say of his failure to capture Lee's army and supplies, my censure should be tempered by the consciousness of the fact that I did not restore him to command for aggressive fighting, but as an organizer and a good hand at defending a position. On complaints about McClellan's failure to crush Lee at Antietam.

* * *

I have no word of encouragement to give! The fact is the people have not yet made up their minds that we are at war with the South. They have not buckled down to the determination to fight this war through; for they have got the idea into their heads that we are going to get out of this fix somehow by strategy! That's the word—strategy! General McClellan thinks he is going to whip the Rebels by strategy; and the Army has got the same notion. To Mary A. Livermore, a clergyman's wife from Chicago, organizing women in Washington to make bandages and other comforts for the Union army.

* * *

The people have not made up their minds that we are at war, I tell you! They think there's a royal road to peace, and that General McClellan is to find it. The army has not settled down to the conviction that we are in a terrible war that has got to be fought out—no; and the officers have not either...Whole regiments have two-thirds of their men absent—a great many by desertion, and a great many on leave granted by company officers, which is almost as bad...The deserters and furloughed men outnumber the recruits. To fill up the army is like undertaking to shovel fleas. You take up a shovelful and before you can dump them anywhere, they are gone. It is like trying to ride a balky horse. You coax, and cheer and spur, and lay on the whip, but you don't get ahead an inch—there you stick. To his group of women organizing aid and relief for sick and wounded soldiers.

* * *

Oh, no, no!...if I should go to shooting men by scores for desertion, I should have such a hullabaloo about my ears as I have not heard yet, and I should deserve it. You cannot order men shot by dozens or twenties. People won't stand it and they ought not to stand it. No, we must change the condition of things some other way. In response to the suggestion that deserters be shot.

* * *

My God! What will the country say? On hearing of Joseph Hooker's defeat at Chancellorsville.

* * *

That's his way. He is always apathetic. When told of General Halleck's apathy about Washington's defenses.

* * *

But how about the soldier? To a doctor giving a medical description of an arm amputation.

* * *

Sherman, do you know why I took a shine to Grant and you?...Well, you never found fault with me. At a meeting with Generals Sherman and Grant about the coming of the end of the war and the desire for a general reconciliation—March 1865.

* * *

Lincoln said he was reminded of a man in Illinois terribly annoyed by a creditor who kept coming often and pressing him to pay the money he owed. Finally the poor debtor saw nothing to do but "to act crazy" whenever asked for money...I have on more than one occasion in this room, when beset by extremists on this question, been compelled to appear very mad. I think no one of you will ever dispose of this subject without getting mad. To Secretary Salmon Chase and Montgomery Blair, one of whom wanted a runaway slave to be taken into the Union army; the other to have him returned to the owner.

* * *

I once heard George Summers tell a story. To Julia Ward Howe, author of the "Battle Hymn of the Republic."

* * *

No commanding general shall do such a thing, upon my responsibility, without consulting me. To Secretary Salmon P. Chase on Major General David Hunter's declaration that

all slaves in Georgia, Florida, and South Carolina are to be "forever free."

* * *

*How much better to thus save the money
which else we sink forever in the war. How
much better to do it while we can, lest the war
ere long render us pecuniarily unable to do it.*
Lincoln's suggestion to buy the slaves and set
them free.

* * *

*I would save the Union. I would save it the
shortest way under the Constitution. The
sooner the national authority can be restored;
the nearer the Union will be the "Union as it
was." If there be those who would not save
the Union, unless they could at the same time
save slavery, I do not agree with them. If there
be those who would not save the Union unless
they could at the same time destroy slavery, I
do not agree with them. My paramount object
in this struggle is to save the Union, and is not
either to save or destroy slavery. If I could save
the Union without freeing any slave, I would*

do it, and if I could save it by freeing all the slaves I would do it; and if I could save it by freeing some and leaving others alone I would also do that. What I do about slavery and the colored race, I do because I believe it helps to save the Union; and what I forbear, I forbear because I do not believe it would help to save the Union. I shall do less whenever I shall believe what I am doing hurts the cause, and I shall do more whenever I shall believe doing more will help the cause. I shall try to correct errors when shown to be errors; and I shall adopt new views so fast as they shall appear to be true views.

I have here stated my purpose according to my view of official duty; and I intend no modification of my often expressed personal wish that all men everywhere could be free. In a letter to the country, August 22, 1862.

* * *

We shall need all the anti-slavery feeling in the country, and more; you can go home and try to bring the people to your views; and you may say anything you like about me, if that will help. Don't spare me...When the hour comes for dealing with slavery, I trust I will be willing to do my duty though it may cost my life. And, gentlemen, lives will be lost. To Reverend Moncure Daniel Conway and the Reverend William Ellery Channing, Unitarian anti-slavery clergymen.

* * *

They are to touch neither a sail nor a pump, but to be merely passengers—dead-heads at that—to be carried snug and dry, throughout the storm, and safely landed right side up...I shall not do more than I can, and I shall do all I can to save the government, which is my sworn duty as well as my personal inclination...I shall do nothing in malice. What I deal with is too vast for malicious dealing. From a letter to a man in New Orleans on those favoring absolute neutrality about states rights and slavery.

* * *

Whereas while heretofore states and nations have tolerated slavery, recently, for the first (time) in the world, an attempt has been made to construct a new nation, upon the basis of, and with the primary and fundamental object to maintain, enlarge and perpetuate human slavery; therefore, resolved, that no such embryo state should ever be recognized by, or admitted into, the family of Christian and civilized nations; and that all Christian and civilized men everywhere should, by all lawful means, resist to the utmost such recognition and admission. To and for John Bright of the British House of Commons to urge Britain and other European nations not to recognize the seceding states.

* * *

Could I get a hundred tolerably intelligent men, with their wives and children, and able to "cut their own fodder" so to speak? Can I have fifty? If I could find twenty-five able-bodied men, with a mixture of women and children,—good things in the family relation, I think,—I could make a successful commencement. I want you to let me know whether this can be done or not. This is the practical part of my wish to see you. To a group of free Negroes called to the White House to discuss Lincoln's idea of colonizing Central American countries or islands with "people of African descent."

* * *

You can tell the President of Hayti that I shan't tear my shirt if he sends a nigger here. To James Redpath, an agent of anti-slavery societies, after Congress recognized the republics of Haiti and Nigeria with the restriction that no black man could be received as a foreign minister.

* * *

I can only trust in God I have made no mistake...It is now for the country and the world to pass judgement on it, and, maybe take action upon it...Yet they are scarcely so great as the difficulties of those who, upon the battle field, are endeavoring to purchase with their blood and their lives the future happiness and prosperity of this country. On September 24, 1862, in announcing the preliminary Emancipation Proclamation from the White House balcony.

* * *

The will of God prevails. In great contests each party claims to act in accordance with the will of God. Both may be, and one must be wrong. God cannot be for and against the same thing at the same time. In the present civil war it is quite possible that God's purpose is something different from the purpose of either party; and yet the human instrumentalities, working just as they do, are the best adaptation to effect his purpose. I am almost ready to say that this is probably true; that God wills this contest, and he wills that it shall not end yet. By his mere great power on the minds of the new contestants, he could have either saved or destroyed the Union without a human contest. Yet the contest began. And having begun he could give the final victory to either side any day. Yet, the contest proceeds. A note left on his desk and copied by Lincoln's secretary John Hay, late September 1862.

* * *

1,200,000 according to the best authority...Yes, sir, 1,200,000—no doubt of it. You see all our generals, when they get whipped, say the enemy outnumbers them from three to five to one, and I must believe them. We have 400,000 men in the field and three times four makes twelve. Don't you see it? When asked how many men the "rebels" had in the field.

* * *

Come, Hatch, I want you to take a walk with me. To Ozias M. Hatch, former secretary of state in Illinois, when Lincoln made a surprise visit to McClellan's Army of the Potomac on October 1, 1862.

* * *

Hatch—Hatch, what is all this? said Lincoln. *Why, Mr. Lincoln, this is the Army of the Potomac,* said Hatch. *No, Hatch, no. This is General McClellan's bodyguard,* said Lincoln. The two men walked back to their tent as the sun was rising.

* * *

Beholders wept at the interview, most of the Confederates even, were moved to tears. A correspondent on Lincoln's visit to a house containing Confederate wounded at Frederick, Maryland.

* * *

Lamon, sing one of your little sad songs. And Ward H. Lamon, Lincoln's friend, sang "Twenty Years Ago," from a poem by Thomas Hood.

* * *

I have just read your dispatch about sore tongued and fatigued horses. Will you pardon me for asking what the horses of your army have done since the Battle of Antietam that fatigues anything? To McClellan's request for more shoes, mules, horses, and other supplies.

* * *

(I feel) somewhat like that boy in Kentucky, who stubbed his toe while running to see his sweetheart. The boy said he was too big to cry and far too badly hurt to laugh. When asked by Colonel John W. Forney about the November election in New York.

* * *

We have lost the elections...(l) The democrats were left in a majority by our friends going to the war. (2) The democrats observed this and determined to re-instate themselves in power, and (3) Our newspapers, by villifying and disparaging the administration, furnished them all the weapons to do it with. Certainly, the ill-success of the war had much to do with this. To Carl Schurz on losing the 1862 elections.

* * *

Sit down and tell me how it is that you, for whose election nobody seemed to hope, are returned with a good majority at your back, while so many of your friends about whom there was no doubt, have been badly beaten. To Congressman William D. Kelley of Philadelphia.

* * *

You need not be surprised to find that that suggestion has been executed any morning. The violent preliminaries to such an event would not surprise me. I have done things lately that must be incomprehensible to the

people, and which cannot now be explained.
To Congressman Kelley who told him that
people approved of the suggestion that Lincoln be found hanging from a lamppost at
the door of the White House.

* * *

We shall see what we shall see. In response
to requests that General McClellan be replaced.

* * *

*I am like the Irishman, I have to do some
things unbeknownst to myself.* Ending the
story of the Irishman in Maine, where state
law prohibited the sale of alcoholic liquor.
Having ordered a glass of lemonade and having the glass set before him, the Irishman
whispered to the druggist, *And now can you
pour in jist a wee drop of the creether unbeknownst to me?*

* * *

*I said I would remove him if he lets Lee's
army get away from him, and I must do so.
He has got the slows.* After a conference where

General McClellan's removal from the Army of the Potomac was demanded.

* * *

Nothing—but it made me think of the man whose horse kicked up and stuck his foot through the stirrup. He said to the horse, "If you are going to get on, I will get off." When asked what he would do about General McClellan's advice on how to carry on the nation's affairs.

* * *

Although you were not successful, the attempt was not an error, nor the failure other than an accident. The courage with which you, in an open field, maintained the contest against the entrenched foe, and the consummate skill and success with which you crossed and re-crossed the river in the face of the enemy, show that you possess all the qualities of a great army, which will yet give victory to the cause of the country and of popular government. Address to the Army of the Potomac after its defeat at Fredericksburg under the newly appointed General Ambrose E. Burnside. In this battle the total Confederate losses were 5,309; the Union losses, 12,653.

* * *

The dogmas of the quiet past are inadequate to the stormy present...As our case is new, so we must think anew, and act anew. We must disenthrall ourselves. From his appeal to Congress to purchase all slaves, using government bonds—late 1862.

* * *

...that will do very well for you, but I am like the starting in Sterne's story, "I can't get out." To Secretary of State Seward whose resignation Lincoln had just received.

* * *

They wish to get rid of me, and I am sometimes half disposed to gratify them...It appears to me the Almighty is against us, and I can hardly see a ray of hope. After a secret caucus of the cabinet.

* * *

Now I have the biggest half of the hog. I shall accept neither resignation. To Senator William P. Fessenden after refusing both Secretary Seward's and Secretary Chase's resignation.

* * *

The division of a State is dreaded as a precedent. But a measure made expedient by a war, is no precedent for times of peace. In approving West Virginia's secession from Virginia to join the Union.

* * *

Suspicions, which may be unjust, need not to be stated. To Congress on the Indian battles along the Minnesota River.

* * *

It is with deep grief that I learn of the death of your kind and brave Father; and, especially, that it is affecting your young heart beyond what is common. In this sad world of ours, sorrow comes to all; and, to the young, it comes with bitterest agony, because it takes them unawares. The older have learned to ever expect it. The memory of your dear Father, instead of an agony, will yet be a sad sweet feeling in your heart, of a purer, and holier sort than you have known before. To Miss Fanny McCullough on the death of her father, Lieutenant Colonel William McCullough, a veteran of the Black Hawk War and commander of the 4th Illinois Cavalry under General Grant.

* * *

These girls are not too old to be kissed. To Commander McCullough whose daughters, Fanny and Nanny, sat on the president's lap.

* * *

There it is, sir! I am to be bullied by Congress, am I? If I do I'll be durned. To Secretary Chase after many, long discussions about the Second Emancipation Proclamation.

* * *

I never, in my life, felt more certain that I was doing right, than I do in signing this paper. But I have been receiving calls and shaking hands since nine o'clock this morning, till my arm is stiff and numb, now this signature is one that will be closely examined, and if they find my hand trembled they will say, "He had some compunctions!" But anyway, it is going to be done. Before signing the Emancipation Proclamation, January 1, 1863.

BY THE PRESIDENT OF THE UNITED STATES OF AMERICA

A Proclamation

Whereas, on the twenty-second day of September, in the year of our Lord one thousand eight hundred and sixty-two, a proclamation was issued by the President of the United States, containing, among other things, the following, to wit:

That on the 1st day of January, A.D. 1863, all persons held as slaves within any State or designated part of a State the people whereof shall then be in rebellion against the United States shall be then, thenceforward, and forever free; and the executive government of the United States, including the military and naval authority thereof, will recognize and maintain the freedom of such persons and will do no act or acts to repress such persons, or any of them, in any efforts they may make for their actual freedom.

That the executive will on the 1st day of January aforesaid, by proclamation, designate the States and parts of States, if any, in which the people thereof, respectively, shall then be in rebellion against the United States; and the fact that any State or the people thereof shall on the day be in good faith represented in the Congress of the United States by members chosen thereto at elections wherein a majority of the qualified voters of such States shall have participated shall, in the absence of strong countervailing testimony, be deemed conclusive evidence that such State and the people thereof are not then in rebellion against the United States.

Now, therefore, I, Abraham Lincoln, President of the United States, by virtue of the power in me vested as Commander-In-Chief of the Army and Navy of the United States in time of actual armed rebellion against the authority and government of the United States, and as a fit and necessary war measure for suppressing said rebellion, do, on this 1st day of January, A.D. 1863, and in accordance with my purpose so to do, publicly proclaimed for the full period of one hundred days from the first day above mentioned, order and designate as the States and parts of States wherein the people thereof, respectively, are this day in rebellion against the United States the following, to wit: Arkansas, Texas, Louisiana (except the parishes of St. Bernard, Palquemines, Jefferson, St. John, St. Charles, St. James, Ascension, Assumption, Terrebone, Lafourche, St. Mary, St. Martin, and Orleans, including the city of New Orleans), Mississippi, Alabama, Florida, Georgia, South Carolina, North Carolina, and Virginia (except the forty-eight counties designated as West Virginia, and also the counties of Berkeley, Accomac, Morthhampton, Elizabeth City, York, Princess Anne, and Norfolk, including the cities of Norfolk and Portsmouth), and which excepted parts are for the present left precisely as if this proclamation were not issued.

And by virtue of the power and for the purpose aforesaid, I do order and declare that all persons held as slaves within said designated States and parts of States are, and henceforward shall be, free; and that the Executive

Government of the United States, including the military and naval authorities thereof, will recognize and maintain the freedom of said persons.

And I hereby enjoin upon the people so declared to be free to abstain from all violence, unless in necessary self-defence; and I recommend to them that, in all case when allowed, they labor faithfully for reasonable wages.

And I further declare and make known that such persons of suitable condition will be received into the armed service of the United States to garrison forts, positions, stations, and other places, and to man vessels of all sorts in said service.

And upon this act, sincerely believed to be an act of justice, warranted by the Constitution upon military necessity, I invoke the considerate judgment of mankind and the gracious favor of Almighty God.

Abraham Lincoln.

Lincoln's signature to Emancipation Proclamation—rarely he wrote his full name.

* * *

Broken eggs cannot be mended. I have is-sued the proclamation (emancipation) and I cannot retract it. In response to criticism.

* * *

They do not want much; they get but little, and I must see them. To Senator Henry Wilson who counselled the president to see fewer people.

* * *

Do you observe this? The rebellion is hard enough to overcome, but there you see some-thing which, in the course of time, will become a greater danger to the republic than the re-bellion itself. To Carl Schurz, on the throng of office seekers and other favors.

* * *

If I have one vice, and I can call it nothing else, it is not to be able to say "No." Thank God for not making me a woman, but if He had, I suppose He would have made me just as ugly as He did, and no one would ever have tempted me. To General Egbert L. Ville.

* * *

Well, young man, if they do, they'll leave behind them a mighty good suit of clothes. To a dandy appointed to a South American consulate, complaining of the bugs in the country he was assigned to, stating that they might eat him up.

* * *

My friend, let me tell you something about that. You are a farmer, I believe, if not, you will understand me. Suppose you had a large cattle yard, full of all sorts of cattle—cows, oxen and bulls—and you kept killing and selling and disposing of your cows and oxen, in one way and another, taking good care of your hills. By and by you would find out that you had nothing but a yard full of old bulls, good for nothing under heaven. Now it will be just so with the army, if I don't stop making brigadier generals. To a man seeking appointment for officer in the army.

* * *

I had rather resign my place and go away from here, if I considered only my personal feelings, but refuse him I must. To Noah

Brooks, his friend and reporter, about an unqualified office seeker.

* * *

Well,—the fact is—the man who has no friends—should be taken care of. When asked by a senator why he didn't fire General Halleck.

* * *

That may all be so, but you must go to your officers about it. To a private complaining about his officers.

* * *

Now, my man, go away, go away! I cannot meddle in your case. I could as easily bail out the Potomac River with a teaspoon as attend to all the details of the army. To the private who repeatedly complained about his officers.

* * *

I look under the bed to see if So and So is there, and if not, I thank heaven and bounce in. To a friend about a pesty office seeker.

* * *

This matter has got to end somehow. Bring me a pair of scales...now put in all the petitions and letters in favor of one man and see how much they weigh, and then weigh the other fellow's fill...make out an appointment for the man who has the heaviest papers. To a clerk, regarding two candidates for a postmastership in Ohio.

* * *

No! I'll have nothing to do with this...there is the door! To a well-dressed man asking to use the president's name in an advertising scheme.

* * *

You know how that Illinois farmer managed the big log that lay in the middle of his field! To the inquiries of his neighbors one Sunday, he announced that he had got rid of the big log. "Got rid of it! How did you do it? It was too big to haul out, too knotty to split and too wet and soggy to burn; what did you do?" "Well, now boys," replied the farmer, "if you won't divulge the secret, I'll tell you how I got rid of it—I plowed around it." Now don't tell anybody, but that's the way I got rid of the governor. I plowed around him, but it took me three mortal hours to do it, and I was afraid every minute he'd see what I was at. To James B. Fry about a complaining governor.

* * *

These cases occurring on the same day, brought me to reflect more attentively than I had before done, as to what is fairly due from us here, in the dispensing of patronage, to-wards the men, who by fighting our battles, bear the chief burden of saving our country. My conclusion is that, other claims and quali-fications being equal, they have the better right; and this is especially applicable to the disabled soldier and the deceased soldier's family. To Postmaster General Montgomery Blair on appointing two widows of fallen sol-diers to postmasterships.

* * *

Colonel, I know your story. But you carry your own condemnation in your face. To a colonel friend who asked to be reinstated after being dismissed for drunkenness.

* * *

I dare not restore this man to his rank and give him charge of a thousand when he puts an enemy into his mouth to steal away his brain. To James M. Scoval in refusing to reinstate a dismissed colonel.

* * *

Well, it is dangerous for an army man to be wandering around without papers to show where he belongs and what he is, but I will see what can be done. To a one-legged soldier on crutches asking for a job.

* * *

Well, then, I can do nothing; for you must know that I have very little influence with this administration. To California Judge Baldwin who was refused a pass to visit his brother in Virginia by both General Halleck and Secretary of War Stanton.

* * *

The only point I make is, there has got to be something done that will be unquestionably in the interest of the Dutch, and to that end I want Schimmelfennig appointed. His name will make up for any difference there may be, and I'll take the risk of his coming out all right— Schim-mel-fen-nig must be appointed. To Stanton, in going over certain applications and recommendations.

* * *

Few things are so troublesome to the government as the fierceness with which the profits in trading are sought. About a speculator who requested a pass to go south to buy cotton.

* * *

Did Stanton say I was a damned fool?...If Stanton said I was a damned fool then I must be one. For he is nearly always right, and generally says what he means. I will step over and see him. To Owen Lovejoy who recommended the mingling of eastern and western troops.

* * *

(Lincoln) always had more hours than oats.
On distributing jobs.

* * *

January 20, 1863, General Burnside
planned a night attack on Lee's army. Rain,
sleet, wind and mud stopped the attack. The
next morning General Hooker talked to the
press about the incompetence of Burnside,
and Lincoln and the government in Washington, calling them imbeciles and stated that a
dictator was needed. Burnside resigned and
on January 25, 1863, Hooker was ordered to
take command of the Army of the Potomac.

* * *

*I do not fear this from the people any more
than I fear assassination from an individual. Now,
to show you my appreciation of what my French
friends would call a coup d'état, let me read you
a letter I have written to General Hooker.* To Chief
of Security Lamon who told Lincoln there was
a scheme to depose him and appoint a dictator.

* * *

That is the most depressing thing about Hooker. It seems to me that he is over-confident. To correspondent Noah Brooks.

* * *

We have here the tail of the Army, so let us get from him how the rank and file feel about matters. To Senator Benjamin F. Wade about a young sergeant who was just granted a pass to Aquia Creek, Virginia.

* * *

It is a great relief to get away from Washington and the politicians. But nothing touches the tired spot. To correspondent Noah Brooks while inspecting the army under General Joseph Hooker at Fredericksburg, Virginia.

* * *

It is about the worst thing I have seen since I am down here. To Noah Brooks about General Hooker's overconfidence.

* * *

"Excuse me, my friend, are you an Episco- palian?" "No, Mr. President, I am a Methodist." "Well, I thought you must be an Episcopalian, because you swear just like Governor Seward, who is a church warden." Communication with the mule driver who drove Lincoln on a corps review.

* * *

General Couch, what do you suppose will become of all these men when the war is over? To General Darius N. Couch while inspecting the troops.

* * *

Write me often. I am very anxious...While I am anxious, please do not think I am impa- tient, or waste a moment's thought on me, to your own hindrance or discomfort. To General Hooker on April 25, 1863, one week after Lincoln's inspection of the army.

* * *

My God! My God! What will the country say! What will the country say! Upon hearing of General Hooker's terrible defeat and withdrawal from Chancellorsville, where General Lee, with half the number, outwitted and outfoxed Hooker.

Losses: Union, 11,000, and Confederates captured, 2,000. Losses: Confederate, 10,000, and Union prisoners taken, 6,000.

* * *

On June 28, 1863, General Joseph Hooker was relieved of his command, and General George Gordon Meade was ordered to take over the command of the Army of the Potomac.

* * *

See what a lot of land these fellows hold, of which Vicksburg is the key...Let us get Vicksburg and the whole country is ours. The war can never be brought to a close until that key is in our pocket. I am acquainted with that region and know what I am talking about. To Commander D. D. Porter.

* * *

One day a delegation headed by a distinguished doctor of divinity from New York, called on me and made the familiar...protest against Grant being retained in his command. After the clergyman had concluded his remarks, I asked if any others desired to add anything to what had already been said. They replied that they did not. Then looking as serious as I could, I said: "Doctor, can you tell me where Grant gets his liquor?" (The doctor seemed to be quite nonplussed, but replied that he could not.) I then said to him: "I am very sorry, for if you could tell me I would direct the Chief Quartermaster of the army to lay in a large stock of the same kind of liquor, and would also direct him to furnish a supply to some of my other generals who have never yet won a victory." To Brigadier General John M. Thayer from Grant's army.

* * *

If I knew what brand of whiskey he drinks I would send a barrel or so to some other generals. Noted by John Nicolay and John Hay when overzealous people complained of Grant's intemperance.

* * *

I think Grant has hardly a friend left, except myself. Noted by John Nicolay.

* * *

The enemy behind us is more dangerous to the country than the enemy before us. To John M. Thayer and others on the bitterness of having Negro regiments in the army.

* * *

I must add that the U.S. government must not...undertake to run the churches...It will not do for the U.S. to appoint trustees...or other agents for the churches. In response to the provost marshal's arrest of the Reverend Dr. Samuel B. McPheeters of St. Louis and the taking control of his church for anti-Unionism—spring 1863.

* * *

He cannot be the next President of the United States unless there shall be a United States to preside over. To the brother of a Democrat intending to run for the presidency—spring 1863.

* * *

Must I shoot a simple-minded soldier boy who deserts, while I must not touch a hair of a wiley agitator who induces him to desert? On the arrest of anti-Union agitators.

* * *

The Government is carrying an immense weight. Untold treasures are in their hands. They are doing the very best they can. Don't badger them. Keep silence, and we'll get you safe across. To an excited delegation of clergymen troubled about the conduct of the war.

* * *

I, Abraham Lincoln, President of the United States, appear of my own volition before this committee of the Senate to say that I, of my own knowledge, know that it is untrue that any of my family hold treasonable communication with the enemy. To the Senate committee investigating the accusation that Mary Todd Lincoln is a Southern spy.

* * *

I do love an open fire; I always had one to home...Whichever way it (the war) ends, I have the impression that I shan't last long after it's over. To author of *Uncle Tom's Cabin*, 1863.

* * *

Last night, about 11 o'clock, I went out to the Soldier's Home alone, riding Old Abe, as you call him (a horse he delighted in riding), and when I arrived at the foot of the hill on the road leading to the entrance of the Home grounds, I was jogging along at a slow gait...when suddenly I was aroused—I may say the arousement lifted me out of my saddle as well as out of my wits—by the report of a rifle, and seemingly the gunner was not fifty yards from where my contemplation ended and my accelerated transit began. My erratic namesake, with little warning...and with one reckless bound...unceremoniously separated me from my eight dollar plug-hat, with which I parted company without my assent, expressed or implied...I can't bring myself to believe that anyone has shot or will deliberately shoot at me with the purpose of killing me; although I must acknowledge that I heard this fellow's bullet whistle at an uncomfortably short distance from these headquarters of mine. I have about concluded that the shot was the result of an accident... To Chief of Security Lamon on an incident which is generally considered an attempt to assassinate the president.

* * *

Why put up the bars when the fence is down all around? If they kill me, the next man will be just as bad for them; and in a country like this, where our habits are simple, and must be, assassination is always possible, and will come if they are determined upon it. In response to demands for greater security for the president.

* * *

Gurowski is the only man who has given me a serious thought of a personal nature. From the known disposition of the man, he is dangerous wherever he may be. I have sometimes thought that he might take my life. It would be just like him to do such a thing. To Chief of Security Lamon on Adam Gurowski, a European republican revolutionary and dismissed translator for the State Department.

* * *

And now, Lord Lyons, go thou and do likewise. To Lord Lyons after reading a long announcement of a royal marriage.

* * *

Just wait now until I sign some papers, that this government may go on. To visitors.

* * *

Boys, I reckon that'll do. We'll shut up shop for the rest of the day. To his secretaries, John Nicolay and John Hay, after an afternoon's work together.

* * *

Dr. Zacharie has operated on my feet with great success, and considerable addition to my comfort. Testimonial for the chiropodist.

* * *

I thought you came here to tell me how to take Richmond. Sit down, my friend, sit down, I am delighted to see you. Lunch with us today, I have not seen enough of you yet. To a stern visitor who completely affirmed Lincoln on how he was running the country.

* * *

Discharge this man. To a congressman's plea in behalf of a sick soldier whose mother had gone insane with worry.

* * *

I'll do the very best I can, the very best I know how, and I mean to keep doing so till the end. If the end brings me out all right, what is said against me won't amount to anything. If the end brings me out wrong, ten angels swearing I was right would make no difference. John Nicolay's note about a day's clamor and confusion.

* * *

You have heard about the man tarred and feathered and ridden out of town on a rail? A man in the crowd asked him how he liked it, and his reply was that if it wasn't for the honor of the thing, he would much rather walk. When an old Illinois friend asked him, one evening, how it felt to be president of the United States.

* * *

I don't know but that God has created some one man great enough to comprehend the whole of this stupendous crisis and transaction from beginning to end, and endowed him with sufficient wisdom to manage and direct it. I confess I do not fully understand, and foresee it all. But I am placed here where I am obliged to the best of my poor ability to deal with it. And that being the case I can only go just as fast as I can see how to go. To Governor Lot M. Morrill.

* * *

If to be the head of Hell is as hard as what I have to undergo here, I could find it in my heart to pity Satan himself. To General Robert C. Schenck.

* * *

That reminds me of a short-legged man in a big overcoat, the tail of which was so long that it wiped out his footprints in the snow. On John Wintrup's signature (a telegraph dispatch operator) to an official letter.

* * *

I've got to let him in, because I promised never to go back on the code. On hearing sharp Morse code raps on the door by son Tad.

* * *

Tell Tad the goats and father are very well, especially the goats. To Mrs. Lincoln on a visit. The two goats were Tad's to play with in the White House.

* * *

Let him run. There's time enough yet for him to learn his letters and get poky. Instructions to Tad's tutor.

* * *

Well, you'll be a man before your mother yet. Bantering with a little boy.

* * *

Bob, it does a man good sometimes to hear the truth. To his son Robert, upon being called a damned old fool on asking a workman a question. *And sometimes I think that's just what I am, a damned old fool.* Again to son Robert.

* * *

I sincerely wish war was a pleasanter and easier business than it is, but it does not admit of holidays. When asked why he took no vacations.

* * *

I wish George Washington or some of the old patriots were here in my place so that I could have a little rest. Observation at his desk.

* * *

Ah, now, I recollect once being engaged in a case of rape, and the counsel for the defence asked the woman why, if, as she said, the rape was committed on a Sunday, she did not tell her husband till the following Wednesday? And the woman answered, "She did not happen to recollect it,"—the case was dismissed at once. When McClellan stated that he forgot to attend a council of war meeting the previous day—as reported by Edward Dicey, an English author.

* * *

...I always want to see and know the men I am riding behind. When asked why he always shook hands with the fireman and conductor of a train.

* * *

He's a thistle! I don't see why God lets him live! About a well-known abolitionist and orator to John Eaton, a Presbyterian chaplain.

* * *

I do not lead, I only follow. To Thomas L. James of Utica, New York.

* * *

I have none. I pass my life preventing the storm from blowing down the tent, and I drive in the pegs as fast as they are pulled up. When asked what his policy was.

* * *

(I am) reminded of an Illinois farmer and his son out in the woods hunting a sow. After a long search they came to a creek branch, where they found hog tracks and signs of a snout rooting, for some distance on both sides of the branch. The old man said to the boy, "Now John, you take up on this side of the branch and I'll go up t'other side, for I believe the old critter is on both sides." In response to being told that a letter of his was used by both sides in a controversy.

* * *

He can compress the most words into the smallest ideas of any man I ever met. An observation of a chatterer.

* * *

(He) mounted the rostrum, threw back his head, shined his eyes, and left the consequences to God. On a Southwestern orator.

* * *

Today I verbally told Col. Worthington that I did not think him fit for a colonel; and now upon his urgent request I put it in writing. To Colonel William H. Worthington who belittled Generals Grant and Sherman.

* * *

The papers are not always reliable, that is to say, Mrs. Welles, they lie and then they re-lie. To Mrs. Gideon Welles who mentioned certain malignant reports in the newspapers.

* * *

It's of no use, madam, for me to go. They do things in their own way over there, and I don't amount to pig tracks in the War Department. To a woman who asked for his influence with that department.

* * *

Oh, there is no alternative but to keep pegging away. When asked what if the war never ended.

* * *

Major-generalships are not as plenty as blackberries. To Illinois sponsors of a proposed major general.

* * *

If we could first know where we are and whither we are tending, we could better judge what to do and how to do it. Observation in the White House.

* * *

For this he especially desires that on this day He whose will, not ours, should ever be done be everywhere remembered and reverenced with profoundest gratitude. The president's announcement of victory at Gettysburg. In this battle the Union lost 23,000 killed, wounded and missing, and the Confederacy, 28,000.

* * *

Drive the invaders from our soil. My God, is that all? Using General George G. Meade's words to the troops for the victory.

* * *

What can we do for the Secretary of the Navy for this glorious intelligence? He is always giving us good news. I cannot, in words, tell you my great joy over this result. It is great, Mr. Welles, it is great. When Secretary of Navy Gideon Welles told Lincoln that Lieutenant General John C. Pemberton had surrendered Vicksburg with 30,000 troops to General Grant on July 7, 1863.

* * *

...In a succession of battles in Pennsylvania, near to us, through three days, so rapidly fought that they might be called one great battle on the 1st, 2nd and 3rd of the month of July; and on the 4th the cohorts of those who opposed the declaration that all men are created equal, "turned tail" and run. Gentlemen, this is a glorious theme, and the occasion for a speech, but I am not prepared to make one worthy of the occasion...I dislike to mention the name of one single officer, lest I might do wrong to those I might forget...Having said this much, I will now take the music. At a serenade for the president after the victories at Gettysburg and Vicksburg.

* * *

I write this now as a grateful acknowledgment for the almost inestimable service you have done the country...I now wish to make the personal acknowledgment that you were right, and I was wrong. To General Grant on July 13, 1863.

* * *

We had them within our grasp. We had only to stretch forth our hands and they were ours. And nothing I could say or do could make the army move. To John Hay, upon hearing that General Meade failed to crush Lee's army after Gettysburg.

* * *

My boy, I have just learned that at a council of war, of Meade and his Generals, it has been determined not to pursue Lee, and now the opportune chance of ending this bitter struggle is lost. To his son Robert who asked his weeping father, "What is the matter, Father?"

* * *

Proclamation of Thanksgiving

July 15, 1863

It has pleased Almighty God to hearken to the supplications and prayers of an afflicted people, and to vouchsafe to the army and navy of the United states victories on land and on the sea so signal and so effective as to furnish reasonable grounds for augmented confidence that the union of these States will be maintained, their Constitution preserved, and their peace and prosperity permanently restored. But these victories have been accorded not without sacrifices of life, limb, health, and liberty, incurred by brave, loyal, and patriotic citizens. Domestic affliction in every part of the country follows in the train of these fearful bereavements. It is meet and right to recognize and confess the presence of the Almighty Father, and the power of his hand equally in these triumphs and in these sorrows.

Now, therefore, be it known that I do set apart Thursday, the 6th day of August next, to be observed as a day for national thanksgiving, praise, and prayer, and I invite the people of the United States to assemble on that *occasion in their customary places of worship, and, in the forms approved by their own consciences, render the homage due to the Divine Majesty for the wonderful things he has done in the nation's behalf, and invoke the influence of his Holy Spirit to subdue the anger which has produced and so long sustained a needless and cruel rebellion, to change the hearts of the insurgents, to guide the counsels of the government with wisdom adequate to so great a national emergency, and to visit with tender care and consolation throughout the length and breadth of our land all those who, through the vicissitudes of marches, voyages, battles, and sieges have been brought to suffer in mind, body, or estate, and finally to lead the whole nation through the paths of repentance and submission to the Divine Will back to the perfect enjoyment of union and fraternal peace.*

* * *

...You have heard of sitting on a volcano. We are sitting upon two; one is blazing away already, and the other will blaze away the moment we scrape a little loose dirt from the

top of the crater. Better let the dirt alone—at least for the present. One rebellion at a time is about as much as we can conveniently handle. To James R. Gilmore in response to the request of appointing a commissioner to investigate the extensive New York City anti-draft riots on July 13, 14, and 16, 1863.

* * *

...Peace does not appear so distant as it did. I hope it will come soon, and come to stay; and so come as to be worth the keeping in all future time. It will then have been proved that, among free men, there can be no successful appeal from the ballot to the bullet; and that they who take such appeal are sure to lose their case, and pay the cost. And then, there will be some black men who can remember that, with silent tongue, and clenched teeth, and steady eye, and well-poised bayonet, they have helped mankind on to this great consummation; while, I fear, there will be some white ones, unable to forget that, with malignant heart, and deceitful speech, they strove to hinder it. Still, let us not be over-sanguine of a speedy, final triumph. Let us be quite sober.

Let us diligently apply the means, never doubting that a just God, in his own good time, will give us the rightful result. Letter to James C. Conkling, read to an immense mass meeting in Springfield, Illinois, in 1863.

* * *

I'm not easily "skeered," but I don't like the looks of the thing. Napoleon has taken advantage of our weakness in our time of trouble, and has attempted to found a monarchy on the soil of Mexico in utter disregard of the Monroe Doctrine. My policy is, attend to one trouble at a time. If we get well out of our present difficulties and restore the Union, I propose to notify Louis Napoleon that it is about time to take his army out of Mexico. When that army is gone, the Mexicans will take care of Maximilian. When asked about the French army in Mexico.

* * *

I desire so to conduct the affairs of this administration that if, at the end, when I come to lay down the reins of power, I have lost every other friend on earth, I shall at least have one friend left, and that friend shall be down inside of me. To a Missouri delegation protesting government policies in their state.

* * *

...I frequently make mistakes myself, in the many things I am compelled to do hastily. To General William S. Rosecrans in Tennessee.

* * *

Proclamation of Thanksgiving

October 3, 1863

The year that is drawing towards its close has been filled with the blessings of fruitful fields and healthful skies. To these bounties, which are so constantly enjoyed that we are prone to forget the source from which they come, others have been added, which are of so extraordinary a nature that they cannot fail to penetrate and soften the heart which is habitually insensible to the ever watchful providence of Almighty God.

In the midst of a civil war of unequalled magnitude and severity, which has sometimes

seemed to foreign states to invite and to pro-
voke their aggression, peace has been pre-
served with all nations, order has been
maintained, the laws have been respected and
obeyed, and harmony has prevailed every-
where, except in the theatre of military con-
flict; while that theatre has been greatly
contracted by the advancing armies and
navies of the Union.

Needful diversions of wealth and strength
from the fields of peaceful industry to the na-
tional defence, have not arrested the plow, the
shuttle, or the ship; the axe has enlarged the
borders of our settlements, and the mines, as
well of iron and coal as of the precious met-
als, have yielded even more abundantly than
heretofore. Population has steadily increased,
notwithstanding the waste that has been made
in the camp, the siege and the battlefield, and
the country, rejoicing in the consciousness of
augmented strength and vigor, is permitted
to expect continuance of years with large in-
crease of freedom.

No human counsel hath devised nor hath
any mortal hand worked out these great
things. They are the gracious gifts of the Most

High God, who, while dealing with us in anger for our sins, hath nevertheless remembered mercy.

It has seemed to me fit and proper that they should be solemnly, reverently, and gratefully acknowledged as with one heart and one voice by the whole American people. I do, therefore, invite my fellow-citizens in every part of the United States, and also those who are at sea and those who are sojourning in foreign lands, to set apart and observe the last Thursday of November next as a day of thanksgiving and praise to our beneficent Father who dwelleth in the heavens. And I recommend to them that, while offering up the ascriptions justly due to Him for such singular deliverances and blessings, they do also, with humble penitence for our national perverseness and disobedience, commend to his tender care all those who have become widows, orphans, mourners or sufferers in the lamentable civil strife in which we are unavoidably engaged, and fervently implore the interposition of the almighty hand to heal the wounds of the nation, and to restore it, as soon as may be consistent with the Divine purposes, to the full enjoyment of peace, harmony, tranquility and Union.

* * *

Edward Everett, the main speaker for the dedication of a National Soldiers' Cemetery at Gettysburg, spoke one hour and 57 minutes.

Abraham Lincoln attended the dedication ceremony and delivered the Gettysburg Address in less than three minutes.

Gettysburg Address

Thursday, November 19, 1863

Fourscore and seven years ago our fathers brought forth on this continent a new nation, conceived in liberty, and dedicated to the proposition that all men are created equal.

Now we are engaged in a great civil war, testing whether that nation, or any nation so conceived and so dedicated, can long endure. We are met on a great battle-field of that war. We have come to dedicate a portion of that field as a final resting-place for those who here gave their lives that that nation might live. It is altogether fitting and proper that we should do this.

But, in a larger sense, we cannot dedicate—we cannot consecrate—we cannot hallow—this ground. The brave men, living and dead, who struggled here, have consecrated it far above our poor power to add or detract. The world will little note nor long remember what we say here, but it can never forget what they did here. It is for us, the living, rather, to be dedicated here to the unfinished work which they who fought here have thus far so nobly advanced. It is rather for us to be here dedicated to the great task remaining before us—that from these honored dead we take increased devotion to that cause for which they gave the last full measure of devotion; that we here highly resolve that these dead shall not have died in vain; that this nation, under God, shall have a new birth of freedom; and that government of the people, by the people, for the people, shall not perish from the earth.

* * *

In our respective parts yesterday, you could not have been excused to make a short address, nor I a long one. I am pleased to know that, in your judgment, the little I did say was not entirely a failure. In response to Edward Everett's affirmation of Lincoln's Gettysburg Address.

* * *

Lovejoy, there is one good thing about this. I now have something I can give everybody. To Owen Lovejoy, while Lincoln was confined to his room with smallpox.

* * *

While I remain in my present position I shall not attempt to retract or modify the Emancipation Proclamation; nor shall I return to slavery any person who is free by the terms of that proclamation. On talk of revoking or amending the Emancipation Proclamation in December 1863.

* * *

Your son Dan has just left me, with my order to the Sec. of War, to administer to him the oath of allegiance, discharge him and send him to you. To Usher F. Linder, an Illinois Democrat, whose son was a war prisoner from the Confederate army—as a Christmas gift, December 26, 1863.

* * *

If people see the Capitol going on, it is a sign we intend the Union shall go on. In response to grumbles about completing the Statue of Freedom atop the Capitol dome during wartime.

* * *

My son, you will never know how gratifying that is to me. No man knows, when that presidential grub gets to gnawing at him, just how deep it will get until he has tried it; and I didn't know but that there was one gnawing at Grant. When informed in the winter of 1863-64 that Ulysses S. Grant had no interest in running for the presidency.

* * * .

General Grant, the nation's appreciation of what you have done, and its reliance upon you for what remains to do, in the existing great struggle, are now presented with this commission, constituting you Lieutenant General in the Army of the United States. In March 1863.

* * *

Now, Mr. Secretary, you know we have been trying to manage this army for nearly three years and you know we haven't done much with it. We sent over the mountains and brought Mr. Grant, as Mrs. Grant calls him, to manage it for us; and now I guess we'd better let Mr. Grant have his own way. To Secretary Edwin M. Stanton in the presence of General Grant.

* * *

I will tell you just what kind of a chap he is. He is one of those long-armed fellows with short legs that can scratch his shins without having to stoop over. When asked his opinion of General Philip H. Sheridan. In the last week of March 1864, Ulysses S. Grant had troops on a line that ran twelve hundred miles from the Atlantic to the Rio Grande with 800,000 men under his command.

* * *

If they can stand it, I guess I can. When told to get out of the rain while Lincoln reviewed troops marching, including several happy Negro regiments.

* * *

A second term would be a great honor and a great labor, which together, perhaps I would not decline if tendered. On being asked about a second term—early 1864.

* * *

Well, it isn't long enough to scare a fellow. On an anti-slavery resolution from the Massachusetts legislature.

* * *

All I can say is, if the radicals want me to lead, let them get out of the way and let me lead. To Anna Elizabeth Dickinson, a 21-year-old vehement and impatient abolitionist, in January 1864.

* * *

Broken eggs cannot be mended; but Louisiana has nothing to do now but to take her place in the union as it was, barring the already broken eggs. The sooner she does so, the smaller will be the amount...past mending. To August Belmont, politically a McClellan Democrat and financially the most eminent Jew in America.

* * *

I am naturally anti-slavery. If slavery is not wrong, nothing is wrong. I can not remember when I did not so think and feel. I claim not to have controlled events, but confess plainly that events have controlled me. If God now wills the removal of a great wrong, and wills also that we of the North as well as you of the South, shall pay fairly for our complicity in that wrong, impartial history will find therein new cause to attest and revere the justice and goodness of God. In a letter to A. G. Hodges of Kentucky, dated April 4, 1864.

* * *

No man knows what that gnawing is till he has had it. To friends about his desire for a second term.

* * *

An editorial in the *Chicago Tribune* in March 1864 states: *A sturdy farmer from Oskaloosa, Iowa, one of the bone and sinew class, called upon us yesterday in relation to business matters. Before leaving, we asked him how Mr. Lincoln stood in Iowa. "Stands?" said the old farmer with glistening eyes and raising his brawny fist. "Old Abe stands seventeen feet higher in Iowa than any other man in the United States!"*

* * *

Do you think, Mr. Carpenter, that you can make a handsome picture of me? To Francis Bicknell Carpenter, a portrait painter, who had been given a six-months' commission by a rich lawyer to produce a painting of Lincoln and his cabinet.

* * *

Well, even if true, I do not see what the rebels would gain by killing or getting possession of me. I am but a single individual and it would not help their cause or make the least difference in the progress of the war. Everything would go right on just the same. When informed by Francis B. Carpenter that a conspiracy existed in Richmond to kidnap or to assassinate the president.

* * *

There is nothing like getting used to things. In response to Carpenter's surprise that Lincoln received weekly threats in the mail.

* * *

Well, it could hardly be otherwise. The cause is that he uses his jaws more than he does his brain. In a discussion with Edward Bates, Salmon Chase, and Jay Cooke on why their fathers' beards were white while the hair on their heads remained its natural color.

* * *

I have never studied the art of paying compliments to women; but I must say that if all that has been said by orators and poets since the creation of the world in praise of women were applied to the women of America, it would not do them justice for their conduct during this war. I will close by saying God bless the women of America. Circa May 1864.

* * *

It is difficult to say a sensible thing nowadays. Spoken at the Philadelphia Sanitary Fair in early 1864. *I claim not to have controlled events, but confess plainly that events have controlled me.* In a letter to Hodges in early 1864. Both these sentences were widely discussed.

* * *

R(aymond), you were brought up on a farm, were you not? Then you know what a chin fly is. My brother and I...were once ploughing corn on a Kentucky farm, I driving the horse, and he holding the plough. The horse was lazy; but on one occasion rushed across the field so that I, with my long legs, could scarcely keep pace with him. On reaching the end of the furrow, I found an enormous chin fly fastened upon him, and knocked him off. My brother asked me what I did that for. I told him I didn't want the old horse bitten in that way. "Why," said my brother, "that's all that made him go." Now, if Mr. Chase has a presidential chin fly biting him, I'm not going to knock him off, if it will only make his department go. To Henry Jarvis Raymond, editor of the *New York Times*, on Secretary of the Treasury Salmon P. Chase's ambitions to become president.

* * *

Well, Mr. Secretary, I don't know unless you give your paper mill another turn. To Secretary Chase's request on what to do about the sinking value of paper money.

* * *

I suppose he will, like the bluebottle fly, lay his eggs in every rotten spot he can find. To John Hay about Chase's constant sniping at Lincoln's performance.

* * *

Salmon P. Chase, secretary of the treasury, is like a horsefly on the neck of a plowhorse. An observation.

* * *

The honorary membership in your association...is gratefully accepted. You comprehend...that the existing rebellion means more...than the perpetuation of African Slavery—that it is, in fact, a war upon the rights of all working people. To the New York Workingmen's Democratic Republican Association in the spring of 1864.

* * *

We all declare for liberty; but in using the same word we do not all mean the same thing. With some the word liberty may mean for each man to do as he pleases with himself, and the product of his labor; while with others the same word may mean for some men to do as they please with other men and the product of other men's labor...The shepherd drives the wolf from the sheep's throat, for which the sheep thanks the shepherd as liberator, while the wolf denounces him for the same act as the destroyer of liberty, especially as the sheep was a black one. Plainly the sheep and the wolf are not agreed upon as a definition of the word liberty; and precisely the same difference prevails today among us human creatures, even

in the North, and all professing to love liberty.
To a Sanitary Fair in Baltimore, April 1864.

* * *

My God! My God! Upon being told of the 26,815 killed and wounded and 4,183 missing in the Battle of the Wilderness around Spotsylvania for 10 days, May 3-13, 1864.

* * *

I feel very much like the man who said he didn't want to die particularly, but if he had got to die, that was precisely the disease he would like to die of...If he takes Richmond, let him have it (the presidency). Upon warning that people might want Ulysses S. Grant for president.

* * *

*Proclamation of a National Day
of Prayer and Fasting
March 30, 1863*

Whereas, the Senate of the United States, devoutly recognizing the Supreme Authority and just Government of Almighty God, in all the affairs of men and of nations, has, by a resolution, requested the President to designate and set apart a day for National prayer and humiliation.

And whereas it is the duty of nations as well as of men, to own their dependence upon the overruling power of God to confess their sins and transgressions, in humble sorrow, yet with assured hope that genuine repentance will lead to mercy and pardon; and to recognize the sublime truth, announced in the Holy Scriptures and proven by all history, that those nations only are blessed whose God is the Lord.

And, insomuch as we know that, by His divine law, nations like individuals are subjected to punishments and chastisements in this world, may we not justly fear that the awful calamity of civil war, which now desolates the land, may be but a punishment, inflicted upon us, for our presumptuous sins, to the needful end of our national reformation as a whole People? We have been the recipients of the choicest bounties of Heaven. We have been preserved, these many years, in peace and prosperity. We have grown in numbers, wealth and power, as no other nation has ever grown. But we have forgotten God. We have forgotten the gracious hand which preserved us in peace, and multiplied and enriched and strengthened us; and we have vainly imagined, in the deceitfulness of our hearts, that all these blessings were produced by some superior wisdom and virtue of our own. Intoxicated with unbroken success, we have become too self-sufficient to feel the necessity of redeeming and preserving grace, too proud to pray to the God that made us!

It behooves us then, to humble ourselves before the offended Power, to confess our national sins, and to pray for clemency and forgiveness. Now, therefore, in compliance with the request, and fully concurring in the views of the Senate, I do, by this my proclamation, designate and set apart Thursday, the 30th. day of April, 1863, as a day of national humiliation, fasting and prayer. And I do hereby request all the People to abstain, on that day, from their ordinary secular pursuits, and to unite, at their several places of public worship and their respective homes, in keeping the day holy to the Lord, and devoted to the humble discharge of the religious duties proper to that solemn occasion.

All this being done, in sincerity and truth, let us then rest humbly in the hope authorized by the Divine teachings, that the united cry of the Nation will be heard on high, and answered with blessings, no less than the pardon of our national sins, and the restoration of our now divided and suffering Country, to its former happy condition of unity and peace.

In witness whereof, I have hereunto set my hand and caused the seal of the United States to be affixed.

Done at the City of Washington, this thirtieth day of March, in the year of our Lord one thousand eight hundred and sixty-three, and of the Independence of the United States the eighty seventh.

By the President: Abraham Lincoln
William H. Seward, Secretary of State.

Senator James Harlan of Iowa introduced this Resolution in the Senate on March 2, 1863. The Resolution asked President Lincoln to proclaim a national day of prayer and fasting. The

Resolution was adopted on March 3, 1863, was signed by Lincoln on March 30, 1863, and designated Thursday, April 30, 1863, as a day of national humiliation, fasting and prayer.

* * *

War at the best, is terrible, and this war of ours, in its magnitude and duration, is one of the most terrible. If I shall discover that General Grant...can be greatly facilitated in (his) work by a sudden pouring forward of men and assistance, will you give them to me? (Cries of) Then I say stand ready, for I am watching for the chance. To a Sanitary Fair in Philadelphia, June 1864.

* * *

Curtin, what do you think of those fellows in Wall Street, who are gambling in gold at such a time as this? For my part, I wish every one of them had his devilish head shot off. To Governor Andrew G. Curtin of Pennsylvania on the gamblers in gold at the expense of Union currency.

* * *

When Grant once gets possession of a place, he holds on to it as if he had inherited it. Visiting General Grant's victories in June 1864.

* * *

Those not skinning can hold a leg. To General Grant on war plans.

* * *

I will neither conceal my gratification, nor restrain the expression of my gratitude... In response to a committee informing him of being renominated at the Republican Convention in Baltimore on June 7, 1864.

* * *

I have not permitted myself, gentlemen, to conclude that I am the best man in the country; but I am reminded, in this connection, of a story of an old Dutch farmer, who remarked to a companion once that "it was not best to swap horses when crossing streams." To a National Union League delegation on June 8, 1864.

* * *

How sleep the brave, who sink to rest
By all their country's wishes blest—
And women o'er the graves shall weep
Where nameless heroes calmly sleep.

Lincoln on the grounds of the Soldiers' Home in late evening.

* * *

As the proverb goes, No man knows so well where the shoe pinches as the man who wears it. To Secretary Chase in disagreement on whom to appoint as assistant secretary of the treasury—June 1864.

* * *

Of all I have said in commendation of your ability and fidelity, I have nothing to unsay; and yet you and I have reached a point of mutual embarrassment in our official relations which it seems cannot be overcome, or longer sustained, consistently with the public service. Finally accepting Secretary Chase's fourth resignation from the Treasury Department—June 1864.

* * *

It is not worth fretting about; it reminds me of an old acquaintance, who, having a son of scientific turn, bought him a microscope. The boy went around experimenting with his glass on everything that came in his way. One day, at the dinner table, his father took up a piece of cheese. "Don't eat that, Father," said the boy. "It is full of wrigglers!" "My son," replied the old gentleman, taking, at the same time, a huge bite, "let 'em wriggle; I can stand it if they can!" In reply to hearing of the agitation in Congress over his pocket veto of its Reconstruction Bill.

* * *

...truth is generally the best vindication against slander. I propose continuing to be myself the judge as to when a member of the cabinet shall be dismissed. In response to jealous infighting among cabinet members.

* * *

The pilots on our western rivers steer from point to point, as they call it—setting the course of the boat no further than they can see. And that is all I propose to do in the great problems that are set before us. On being blamed for inflation, as well as political and military reverses, in August 1864.

* * *

What is the presidency worth to me if I have no country? Amid general discontent with the war, the economy, and the draft.

* * *

Well, it was named after I was. In answer to the question of whether the town of Lincoln, Illinois, was named after him.

* * *

I have faith in the people. They will not consent to disunion. The danger is, in their being misled. Let them know the truth and the country is safe...Things look badly and I can't avoid anxiety...I feel a presentiment that I shall not outlast the rebellion. When it is over, my work will be done. To a *Boston Journal* reporter.

* * *

I am much indebted to the good Christian people of the country for their constant prayers and consolations...The purposes of the Almighty are perfect, and must prevail, though we erring mortals may fail... To Eliza P. Gurney, a Quaker.

* * *

They must nominate a Peace Democrat on a war platform, or a War Democrat on a peace platform; and I personally can't say that I care much which they do. To Noah Brooks, his friend and reporter, just before the Democratic Convention in Chicago, August 29, 1864.

* * *

Gentlemen, it is generally the case that a man who begins a work is not the best man to carry it on to a successful termination. I believe it was so in the case of Moses, wasn't it? He got the children of Israel out of Egypt, but the Lord selected somebody else to bring them to their journey's end. A pioneer has hard work to do, and generally gets so battered and splattered that people prefer another, even though they may accept the principle. To Reverend Dr. Moncure Conway and some associates.

* * *

I expect the friends of George B. McClellan manage their side of this contest in their own way, and I will manage my side of it in my way. To a group of McClellan Democrats delivering their protests to Lincoln.

* * *

It is better that we both should be beaten than the forces in front of the enemy should be weakened or perhaps defeated on account of the absence of these men. In response to suggestions that soldiers be furloughed to vote.

* * *

I remember a good story when I hear it, but I never invented anything original. I am only a retail dealer. To Noah Brooks.

* * *

I suppose the institution of slavery really looks small to him. He is so put up by nature, that a lash upon his back would hurt him, but a lash upon anybody else's back does not hurt him. Of a political antagonist's indifference to slavery.

* * *

Like the man in an open buggy caught at night on a country road in a heavy downpour of rain. He was hurrying to shelter, passing a farmhouse where a man somewhat drunk put his head out of a window and yelled, "Hullo! Hullo!" The traveler stopped his buggy in the rain and asked what was wanted. "Nothing of you," came the voice at the window. "Well, what in the damnation do you yell hullo for when people are passing?" "Well, what in the damnation are you passing for when people are yelling hullo?" A Lincoln joke.

* * *

Oh, I don't have to. You know I have Stanton in my cabinet. In reply to the observation that he never swore.

* * *

The question was, "Why does man have breasts?" After a long debate was submitted to the presiding judge who wisely decided that if under any circumstances, however fortuitous, or by any chance or freak, no matter what the nature or by what cause, a man should have a baby, there would be the breasts to nurse it. When asked why General McClellan fortified the north of Washington.

* * *

(Like) an Illinois farmer who for years had loved and prized a soaring elm tree, that spread its branches near his house. One day, the farmer saw a squirrel scurry up the giant elm's trunk and suddenly disappear in a hole. Looking further, he found the great tree hollow the whole inside rotten and ready to fall. "My God! I wish I had never seen that squirrel and I wish we had never seen what we have seen today." Seeing copies of dispatches of shocking disloyalties, names, and individuals.

* * *

A man chased around a tree by a bull gained on the bull and caught it by the tail.

The bull pawed, snorted, broke into a run; the man after it still holding to the tail and bawling, "Darn you, who commenced this fuss?" Told to Lamon, his chief of security, about the conflict between the North and the South.

* * *

Say to them, that I have Jeff Davis by the throat. When asked for a message to the 10th Illinois Cavalry.

* * *

Whenever a guest was dying in his house, he carried him out to die in the street. About a St. Louis hotelkeeper who claimed no one ever died in his hotel.

* * *

Like a man out West who put his boy inside a barrel to hold up the head while the father pounded down the hoops. When the job was done, the father saw that he hadn't figured on how to get the boy out again. "Some people can succeed better in getting themselves and others corked up than in getting uncorked." On a general who was outmaneuvered.

* * *

Like two dogs that get less eager to fight the nearer they come to each other. On Union and Confederate armies' maneuvering.

* * *

When I get this handkerchief out of this coat-tail pocket I intend to shake hands with you boys! To a Pennsylvania infantry company on a visit to the president.

* * *

A man enters the theater first as the curtain goes up. So interested is the man in looking at what is happening on the stage that he puts his tall silk hat, open side up, on the seat next to him, without noticing a very stout woman who is nearsighted. She sits down. There is a crumbling noise. The owner of the flattened hat reaches out for it as the stout woman rises. He looks at his hat, looks at her: "Madam, I could have told you that my hat wouldn't fit you before you tried it on." A story.

* * *

Mr. Arnold, if I could not get momentary respite from the crushing burden I am constantly carrying, my heart would break. To Senator Isaac N. Arnold who asked him how he could indulge in levity amid so much sorrow and many reverses.

* * *

Tweet, tweet, tweet, isn't it singing sweetly? Imitating a bird singing in a tree outside the window, immediately after Leonard Swett, an old Illinois friend, narrated a dirge of gloom and doom, and recommendations—summer 1864.

* * *

I don't agree with you. I am not at all concerned about that, for we know that the Lord is always on the side of right. But it is my constant anxiety and prayer that I and this nation should be on the Lord's side. To a minister and his delegation who "hoped the Lord is on our side."

* * *

To run down all the suspicious insinuations, inveracities, innuendoes, uttered against a man in my place would be a perpetual flea hunt. Lincoln's response to newspaper reports.

* * *

My faith is greater than yours. But I also believe He will compel us to do right in order that He may do these things, not so much because we desire them as that they accord with His plans of dealing with this nation, in the midst of which He means to establish justice. I think He means that we shall do more than we have yet done in furtherance of His plans, and He will open the way for our doing it. I have felt His hand upon me in great trials and submitted to His guidance, and I trust that as He shall further open the way I will be ready to walk therein, relying on His help and trusting in His goodness and wisdom. Sometimes it seems necessary that we should be confronted with perils which threaten us with disaster in order that we may not get puffed up and forget Him who has much work for us yet to do. To an Iowa delegation.

* * *

The only thing to do is to keep pegging away. To a man visiting the White House.

* * *

I am a tired man, sometimes I am the tiredest man on earth. To a Michigan woman.

* * *

I would rather be defeated with the soldier behind me than to be elected without it. To Henry E. Wing, a *New York Tribune* reporter.

* * *

Glad to see you looking so well, boys, glad to meet you. In reviewing troops as Lincoln dismounted from his horse and shook hands with thousands.

* * *

Conner, I can't overrule Stanton, but I need a special commissioner to go among the rank and file of the army to find out what the soldiers of this country think of the government in its greatest crisis. Conner, will you be a special commissioner? To Jim Conner who had been refused a pass by Stanton to visit four sons and other neighbor boys in the Army of the Potomac.

* * *

Well, I don't believe shooting will do him any good. Give me that pen. In response to a plea to commute the death sentence of a soldier.

* * *

That's bad, very bad. On an army surgeon's court-martial for drunkenness. *That's bad, too. An officer shouldn't insult a lady, by any means.* The same case indicting the same officer for insulting a lady. *Really. I don't know about this. There are exceptions to every rule but as a general thing it's very hard to insult a lady by kissing her. But it seems the doctor only attempted to kiss her—perhaps the insult consisted in his not fully succeeding. I don't know as I ought to interfere in behalf of a man who attempts to kiss a lady and doesn't do it,...We can easily dispose of the kissing part, but I must look into the drunkenness a little. I can't overlook that. I'll have to get good evidence that it was strictly a New Year's offence, and is not a common occurrence with the doctor.* The case was taken under advisement.

* * *

Better give your path to a dog, than be bitten by him in contesting for the right. Even killing the dog would not cure the bite. To Captain James Madison Cutts whose court-martial for insubordination and window peeping in a hotel was commuted by President Lincoln. Captain Cutts in later battles won the "Medal of Honor of the United States" for extraordinary bravery.

* * *

Send him to her by all means. To the secretary of war in response to a Quaker girl who wanted her boyfriend sent home because on a furlough home to vote "we very foolishly indulged too fully in matrimonial matters."

* * *

I want to punish the young man—probably in less than a year he will wish I had withheld the pardon. We can't tell, though, I suppose when I was a young man I should have done the same fool thing. In granting pardon to a condemned deserter who went home to marry his girl, who was being assiduously wooed by another.

* * *

What, madam, do I not destroy them when I make them my friends? To an elderly woman who voiced concern over Lincoln's kind words about the enemy.

* * *

If your son never looks on death till further orders come from me to shoot him, he will live to be a great deal older than Methuselah. To an old man complaining that his son, instead of receiving pardon from death, received the sentence that the son "was not to be shot until further orders from me."

* * *

My poor girl, you have come with no governor, or senator or member of Congress, to plead your cause. You seem honest and truthful, and

*you don't wear hoops; and I'll be whipped but
I'll pardon your brother.* To a young woman
in a neat, plain dress.

* * *

*But I put it to you, and I leave it for you to
decide for yourself; if Almighty God gives a
man a cowardly pair of legs how can, how
can he help their running away with him?* To
Judge Advocate General Joseph Holt about a
soldier, in the heat of battle, throwing away
his gun and hiding behind a tree stump.

* * *

*Tell him I will not see him. I cannot. Don't
ask me again. Tell him I have read the papers
in the case, all of them, fully, word for word.
The boy deserted three times, the last time
when on guard at Washington and he cannot
be pardoned. I will not interfere. He must be
shot.* To John Hay who relayed a message from
the boy's father.

* * *

*Well, I will pardon your husband and turn
him over to you for safe keeping.* The woman

broke into uncontrollable tears. *My dear woman, if I had known how badly it was going to make you feel, I never would have pardoned him.* The woman sobbed still more and told Lincoln that he didn't understand her. *Yes, yes, I do, and if you don't go away at once I shall be crying with you.* To a Northern woman whose husband had fought for the Confederacy with Mosby's Rangers.

* * *

Don't kneel to me, but thank God and go. To a woman who knelt to give thanks for the release of her husband.

* * *

I'm afraid with all my troubles I shall never get to the resting-place you speak of. But if I do, I am sure I shall find you. That you wish me to get there is, I believe, the best wish you could make for me. Good-by. To a woman who hoped to see Lincoln in heaven, after granting a suspension of execution for her husband.

* * *

I could not think of going into eternity with the blood of that poor young man on my skirts. It is not to be wondered at that a boy, raised on the farm, probably in the habit of going to bed at dark, should, when required to watch, fall asleep; and I cannot consent to shooting him for such an act. On a 19 year old who fell asleep on picket duty.

* * *

Well, I have made one family happy, but I don't know about the discipline of the army! While signing a reprieve.

* * *

Please suspend execution in any and all sentences of death in your department until further orders. To General Benjamin F. Butler at Fortress Monroe.

* * *

Voorhees, don't it seem strange to you that I, who could never so much as cut off the head of a chicken, should be elected, or selected, into the midst of all this blood? To

Indiana Democratic Congressman Daniel W. Voorhees.

* * *

Yes—but I am sometimes reminded of Old Mother Partington or the sea beach. A big storm came up and the waves began to rise till the water came in under her cabin door. She got a broom and went to mopping it out. But the water rose higher and higher, to her knees, to her waist, at last to her chin. But she kept on sweeping and exclaiming, "I'll keep on sweeping as long as the broom lasts, and we will see whether the storm or the broom will last the longest." To Ralph Emerson who told Lincoln, "The great West is with you." In the 1864 elections.

* * *

Remember, Dick, to keep close to the people—they are always right and will mislead no one. To Dick Oglesby running for governor in Illinois in 1858.

* * *

Yes, I have. And I don't think much of a man who is not wiser today than he was yesterday. To Congressman John B. Alley, accusing Lincoln of changing his policies.

* * *

This thing reminds me of a story I read in a newspaper the other day. It was of an Italian captain, who ran his vessel on a rock and knocked a hole in her bottom. He set his men to pumping and he went to prayers before a figure of the Virgin in the bow of the ship. The leak gained on them. It looked at last as if the vessel would go down with all on board. The captain, at length, in a fit of rage at not having his prayers answered, seized the figure of the Virgin and threw it overboard. Suddenly the leak stopped, the water was pumped out, and the vessel got safely into port. When docked for repairs, the statue of the Virgin Mary was found stuck headforemost in the hold...I don't intend precisely to throw the Virgin Mary overboard, and by that I mean the Constitution, but I will stick it in the hole if I can. These rebels are violating the Constitution to destroy the Union. I will violate the Constitution, if necessary, to save the Union, and I suspect...that our Constitution is going to have a rough time of it before we get done with this row. Now, what I want to know is, whether, Constitution aside, this project of issuing interest-bearing notes is a good one! To Secretary of Treasury Chase in a discussion about raising money.

* * *

It is no secret that I have wished, and still do wish, mankind everywhere to be free. To a torchlight procession of hundreds of Negroes on the White House lawn amid great cheering and cries of "God bless Abraham Lincoln."

* * *

Well, I have got that job busted out, now I guess I will go over to the War Department before I go to bed, and see if there is any news. To Francis B. Carpenter, the portrait painter, late at night, after Lincoln finished signing documents.

* * *

Whose boots did you think I blacked? To Senator Charles Sumner who asked him, *Mr. President, do you black your own boots?*

* * *

Oh, I guess not—I couldn't rest and thought I'd take a walk. To a worrisome guard who asked Lincoln whether it wasn't risky to be out alone at night.

* * *

He came pretty near getting away with me, didn't he? He got the bit in his teeth before I could draw rein. To Nichols, his guard, who helped quiet the horse that Lincoln was riding after the second assassination attempt. The bullet went through his top hat and ricocheted off it.

* * *

But I can't run this thing on the theory that every officeholder must think I am the greatest man in the nation. To Chief of Security Lamon who complained about two office appointees speaking meanly of the president.

* * *

There are too many pigs for the tits. On the many office seekers.

* * *

I hain't got anything to give you. To a man who wanted the position of inspector of army horses.

* * *

I hate to have old friends like the Senator go away. And another thing I usually find out is that a Senator or Representative out of business is a sort of lame duck. He has to be provided for. A senator introducing his successor, asking to be appointed commissioner of Indian Affairs. This is, it seems, the origin of "lame duck" political lingo.

* * *

I shall never be glad anymore. To Mrs. Louis Powell Harvey, wife of the governor of Wisconsin, whose husband drowned while moving supplies for the soldiers wounded in the Battle of Shiloh.

* * *

I only wish to say to you that an order, which is equivalent to the granting of a hospital in your state, has been issued from the War Department, nearly twenty-four hours. To Mrs. Harvey after her repeated and tearful petitions for veterans' hospitals in the North.

* * *

I am just enough of a politician to know that there was not much doubt about the result of the Baltimore Convention; but about this thing I am very far from being certain. I wish I were certain. To Noah Brooks, his reporter friend, on election day, November 8, 1864.

* * *

She is more anxious than I. In sending favorable early election returns to his wife from the telegraph office on the second floor of the War Department.

* * *

You have more of that feeling of personal resentment than I. To Gustavus Vasa Fox's glee over two beaten opponents.

* * *

Perhaps I may have too little of it, but I never thought it paid. A man has no time to spend half his life in quarrels. If any man ceases to attack me, I never remember the past against him. To John Hay on feeling resentment.

* * *

Dana, have you ever read any of the writings of Petroleum V. Nasby? ...Let me read you a specimen. To Assistant Secretary of War Charles A. Dana, in a lull of election returns.

* * *

I earnestly believe that the consequences of this day's work, if it be as you assure me and as now seems probable, will be to the lasting advantage, if not to the very salvation, of the country...I do not impugn the motives of any one opposed to me. It is no pleasure to me to triumph over any one; but I give thanks to the Almighty for this evidence of the people's resolution to stand by free government and the rights of humanity. To serenaders with a brass band cheering as Lincoln left the War Department at 2:00 p.m. on November 9, 1864.

Lincoln won his second term by over 400,000 votes, or 55.09 percent of the votes, to McClellan's 44.91 percent. The electoral vote was 212 for Lincoln, and 21 for McClellan.

* * *

Lincoln's speech from the north portico of the White House after his reelection:

It has long been a grave question whether any government, not too strong for the liberties of its people, can be strong enough to maintain its own existence, in great emergencies. On this point the present rebellion brought our republic to a severe test...the election was a necessity. We can not have free government without elections; and if the rebellion could force us to forego, or postpone, a national election, it might fairly claim to have already conquered and ruined us...Human-nature will not change. In any future great national trial, compared with the men of this, we shall have as weak, and as strong "as silly and as wise" as bad and good...Gold is good in its place; but living, brave, patriotic men are better than gold. So long as I have been here I have not willingly planted a thorn in any man's bosom.

*While I am deeply sensible to the high compli-
ment of a re-election; and duly grateful, as I
trust, to Almighty God for having directed my
countrymen to a right conclusion, as I think, for
their own good, it adds nothing to my satisfac-
tion that any other man may be disappointed
or pained by the result...And now, let me close
by asking three hearty cheers for our brave
soldiers and seamen and their gallant and
skillful commanders.* To a roaring, cheering
crowd on the White House lawn on the night
of November 10, 1864.

* * *

*Will you do me the favor to leave that paper
with me? I want it in order that, if I appoint Mr.
Chase, I may show the friends of the other
persons for whom the office is solicited by how
powerful an influence and by what strong
personal recommendations the claims of Mr.
Chase were supported...And I want the paper
also in order that, if I should appoint any other
person, I may show his friends how powerful
an influence and what strong personal recommendations I was obliged to disregard in
appointing him.* To a Philadelphia delegation

with a signed petition for Salmon P. Chase's appointment to the Supreme Court.

* * *

Mr. Chase is a very able man. He is a very ambitious man and I think on the subject of the presidency a little insane. He has not always behaved very well lately and people say to me, "Now is the time to crush him out." Well, I'm not in favor of crushing anybody out! If there is anything that a man can do and do it well, I say let him do it. Give him a chance. To Richard Henry Dana and Judge E. R. Hoar on Lincoln's intentions about appointing Chase to the Supreme Court.

* * *

I believe I shall never be old enough to speak without embarrassment when I have (nothing) to talk about. I have no good news to tell you and yet I have no bad news to tell...The most interesting news we now have is from Sherman. We all know where he went in at, but I can't tell where he will come out at. I will now close by proposing three cheers for

General Sherman and his army. To a serenading party, December 6, 1864.

* * *

Say to General Sherman, for me, whenever and wherever you see him, "God bless him and God bless his army." That is as much as I can say, and more than I can write. To Colonel A. H. Markland leaving with mail for Sherman's army, which was "lost sight" of for 32 days and marched three hundred miles from Atlanta to Savannah, consuming or destroying everything in its path.

* * *

I know what hole he went in at, but I can't tell what hole he will come out of. Two weeks after General William T. Sherman's disappearance.

* * *

When you were about leaving Atlanta for the Atlantic coast, I was anxious, if not fearful; but feeling that you were the better judge, and remembering that "nothing risked, nothing gained" I did not interfere. Now, the undertaking being a success, the horror is all yours;

for I believe none of us went further than to acquiesce...Please make my grateful acknowledgments to your whole army, officers and men. To General Sherman on December 26, 1864, in response to Sherman's telegram, "I present to you as a Christmas gift, the city of Savannah..."

* * *

Whatever others may say or do, I never can, and never will, be accessory to such treatment of human beings. When asked to retaliate for the inhuman treatment of prisoners of war in the South, especially at Chancellorsville.

* * *

Good evening, Mars. To Secretary of War Edwin M. Stanton at the doorway of Lincoln's study.

* * *

I have made up my mind to make very few changes in the offices, which is my gift for my second term. I think, now, that I shall not move a single man, except for delinquency. To remove a man is very easy, but when I go to fill his place, there are twenty applicants, and of these I must make nineteen enemies. To a caller asking about a shake-up of the cabinet for the new term.

* * *

Neither would I. But it was a time when a man with a policy would have been fatal to the country. I have never had a policy, I have simply tried to do what seemed best as each day came. To John M. Palmer, an Illinois Union Democrat, who chided Lincoln about the country electing from a "little one-horse town a one-horse lawyer" for president, while Lincoln was being shaved and his face all lathered.

* * *

Letter to Mrs. Lydia Bixley, 15 Dover Street, Boston, Massachusetts:

I have been shown in the files of the War Department a statement of the Adjutant General of Massachusetts, that you are the mother of five sons who have died gloriously on the field of battle.

I feel how weak and fruitless must be any words of mine which should attempt to beguile you from the grief of a loss so overwhelming. But I cannot refrain from tendering to you the consolation that may be found in the thanks of the Republic they died to save.

I pray that our Heavenly Father may assuage the anguish of your bereavement, and leave you only the cherished memory of the loved and lost, and the solemn pride that must be yours, to have laid so costly a sacrifice upon the altar of Freedom. Yours, very sincerely and respectfully,

A. LINCOLN.

* * *

On Thursday two ladies from Tennessee came before the president, asking the release of their husbands held as prisoners of war at Johnson's Island. They were put off till Friday, when they came again, and were again put off to Saturday. At each of the interviews one of the ladies urged that her husband was a religious man. On Saturday the president ordered the release of the prisoners, and then said to this lady, *You say your husband is a religious man; tell him when you meet him, that I say I am not much of a judge of religion, but that, in my opinion, the religion that sets men to rebel and fight against their government, because, as they think, that government does not sufficiently help some men to eat their bread on the sweat of other men's faces, is not the sort of religion upon which people can get to heaven!*

* * *

Don't wait to send it to California in your correspondence. I've a childish desire to see it in print right away. To Noah Brooks on the above letter, which was published in the *Washington Chronicle* and widely reprinted.

* * *

THE THIRTEENTH AMENDMENT OF THE U.S. CONSTITUTION

Section 1. Neither slavery nor involuntary servitude, except as a punishment for crime whereof the party shall have been duly convicted, shall exist within the United States, or any place subject to their jurisdiction.

Section 2. Congress shall have power to enforce this article by appropriate legislation.

* * *

This ends the job. I feel proud that Illinois is a little ahead...There is a task yet before us—to go forward and consummate by the votes of the States that which Congress so nobly began yesterday...They will do it. On February 1, 1865, when hearing that Illinois had ratified the Thirteenth Amendment to the Constitution, which passed Congress on January 31, 1864, outlawing slavery or involuntary servitude in the United States of America.

* * *

He could strut while sitting down. On relieving General Benjamin F. Butler of his command.

* * *

Let nothing which is transpiring, change, hinder, or delay your military movements or plans. To Ulysses S. Grant on February 1, 1865, while peace talks were in progress.

* * *

Never have I seen so small a nubbin come out of so much husk. A remark about 90-pound Alexander Stephens of Georgia shedding his overcoat and wrappings aboard the steamer for peace talks with the president in February 1865.

* * *

Well, Stephens, there has been nothing we could do for our country. Is there anything I can do for you personally? To Alexander Stephens as the Southern peace commission was about to leave the failed peace talks. Stephens asked for the release of his nephew from prison, and Lincoln granted the release.

* * *

You had better take that along. It is considered quite a curiosity down your way, I believe. Handing Confederate Lieutenant Stephens a pass and a picture of himself, having obtained release from imprisonment.

* * *

Mr. Moorhead, haven't you lived long enough to know that two men may honestly differ about a question and both be right? To Representative James K. Moorhead who

demanded hangings of rebel leaders and total retaliation against the South in February
1865.

* * *

*I have known Andy for many years. He
made a bad slip the other day, but you need
not be scared. Andy ain't a drunkard.* To Hugh
McCulloch on Vice President Andrew Johnson's
sorry and drunken performance at the inaugural on March 4, 1865.

* * *

Second Inaugural Address
March 4, 1865

*Fellow Countrymen: At this second appear-
ing to take the oath of the presidential office,
there is less occasion for an extended address
than there was at the first. Then a statement,
somewhat in detail, of a course to be pursued,
seemed fitting and proper. Now, at the expi-
ration of four years, during which public dec-
larations have been constantly called forth on
every point and phase of the great contest
which still absorbs the attention and engrosses*

the energies of the nation, little that is new could be presented. The progress of our arms, upon which all else chiefly depends, is as well known to the public as to myself; and it is, I trust, reasonably satisfactory and encouraging to all. With high hope for the future, no prediction in regard to it is ventured.

On the occasion corresponding to this four years ago, all thoughts were anxiously directed to an impending civil war. All dreaded it—all sought to avert it. While the inaugural address was being delivered from this place, devoted altogether to saving the Union without war, insurgent agents were in the city seeking to destroy it without war—seeking to dissolve the Union, and divide effects, by negotiation. Both parties deprecated war; but one of them would make war rather than let the nation survive; and the other would accept war rather than let it perish. And the war came.

One-eighth of the whole population were colored slaves, not distributed generally over the Union, but localized in the Southern part of it. These slaves constituted a peculiar and powerful interest. All knew that this interest was, somehow, the cause of the war. To *strengthen, perpetuate, and extend this inter-est was the object for which the insurgents would rend the Union, even by war; while the government claimed no right to do more than to restrict the territorial enlargement of it.*

Neither party expected for the war the magnitude or the duration which it has already attained. Neither anticipated that the cause of the conflict might cease with, or even be-fore, the conflict itself should cease. Each looked for an easier triumph, and a result less fundamental and astounding. Both read the same Bible, and pray to the same God; and each invokes his aid against the other. It may seem strange that any men should dare to ask a just God's assistance in wringing their bread from the sweat of other men's faces; but let us judge not, that we be not judged. The prayers of both could not be answered—that of nei-ther has been answered fully.

The Almighty has his own purposes. "Woe unto the world because of offenses! for it must needs be that offenses come; but woe to that man by whom the offense cometh." If we shall suppose that American slavery is one of those offenses which, in the providence of God, must needs come, but which, having continued through his appointed time, he now wills to remove, and that he gives to both North and South this terrible war, as the woe due to those by whom the offense came, shall we discern therein any departure from those divine attributes which the believers in a living God always ascribe to him? Fondly do we hope— fervently do we pray—that this mighty scourge of war may speedily pass away. Yet, if God wills that it continue until all the wealth piled by the bondman's two hundred and fifty years of unrequited toil shall be sunk, and until every drop of blood drawn with the lash shall be paid by another drawn with the sword, as was said three thousand years ago, so still it must be said, "The judgments of the Lord are true and righteous altogether."

With malice toward none; with charity for all; with firmness in the right, as God gives us to see the right, let us strive on to finish the work we are in: to bind up the nation's wounds; to care for him who shall have borne the battle, and for his widow, and his orphan—to do all which may achieve and cherish a just and lasting peace among ourselves, and with all nations.

At the end of the address there were "many moist eyes and tears coursing down faces unashamed."

* * *

Verses from the fifth chapter of Isaiah:

None shall he weary nor stumble among them; none shall slumber nor sleep; neither shall the girdle of their loins be loosed, nor the latchet of their shoes be broken:

Whose arrows are sharp, and all their bows bent, their horses' hoofs shall be counted like flint, their wheels like a whirlwind.

Where Lincoln kissed the Bible.

* * *

Everyone likes a compliment. (I expect it.) *to wear as well as—perhaps better than—anything I have produced; but I believe it is not immediately popular. Men are not flattered by being shown that there has been a difference of purpose between the Almighty and them.*

Written to Thurlow Weed, thanking him for "good words" on his Second Inaugural Address.

* * *

Why should they do it? How can they? Upon seeing the damage of souvenir seekers the night of the inauguration in the White House.

* * *

When I get through with such a day's work there is only one word that can express my condition, and that is—flabbiness. To Noah Brooks after a day of meeting senators and scrub-women—all seeking favors or jobs.

* * *

Please read and answer this letter as though I was not President, but only a friend. My son, now in his twenty-second year, having graduated at Harvard, wishes to see something of the war before it ends. I do not wish to put him in the ranks, nor yet to give him a commission, to which those who have already served long, are better entitled, and better qualified to hold. Could he, without embarrassment to you, or detriment to the service, go into your military family with some nominal rank, I, and not the public, furnishing his necessary means? If so, say so without the least hesitation, because I am as anxious, and as deeply interested, that you shall not be encumbered as you can be yourself. To Ulysses S. Grant. Robert Lincoln was accepted and received the rank of captain and assistant adjutant general, and he performed well and was equally well accepted, having many of the genial traits of his father.

* * *

Now, Henderson, remember you are responsible to me for those men. If they do not behave, I shall have to put you in prison for their sins. To Senator John B. Henderson of Missouri whose two lists of prisoners were pardoned by Lincoln.

* * *

Let no depredation be committed upon the property or possessions of the Sisters of Charity of Nazareth Academy. An order to Bardstown, Kentucky—indicating, too, that provisions for their hospitals in Chicago and Washington be charged to the War Department.

* * *

No man knows the distress of my mind. To Brownwell of Illinois on the many appeals for pardons or leniency—February 1865.

* * *

No, Mrs. Stowe, I shall never live to see peace. This war is killing me. To Harriet Beecher Stowe, on observing that the war was coming to a close.

* * *

Grant has the bear by the hind leg while Sherman takes off the hide. To a White House caller on their war strategy.

* * *

...that reminds me of the horse dealer in Kentucky who got baptized in the river. The ceremony once over he insisted on it a second time. The preacher hesitated, but the horse

trader had his way. And when he came up from the second ducking he gasped, "There now! Now I can tell the devil to go hell." To a caller on Generals Grant and Sherman's encirclement of General Lee.

* * *

You are not to decide, discuss or confer upon any political questions. Such questions the President holds in his own hands, and will submit them to no military conferences or conventions. Message to Grant about peace terms.

* * *

Never for a moment. When asked by Grant whether he ever doubted the final success of the cause, while visiting Grant on the front where Lincoln saw the horrors of battle.

* * *

Kitties, thank God you are cats, and can't understand this terrible strife that is going on. Stroking two little orphan kittens on his lap at the front with Grant.

* * *

Good-by, gentlemen. God bless you all! Remember, your success is my success. To Grant, his officers and troops, ending his visit to the front on March 29, 1865, Lincoln spoke in a broken voice.

* * *

Why not, my boy! That's just where I do want to go. When told by Dr. Jerome Walker that he would not want to visit sick rebel soldiers in a tent.

* * *

I hope a Confederate Colonel will not refuse me his hand. Extending his hand to seriously wounded Colonel Harry L. Benbow, who fought four years with the Confederacy. They warmly shook hands.

After visiting a hospital with five thousand sick and wounded from both sides, Lincoln, arm weary, was offered a drink. He took a glass of lemonade.

* * *

Don't kneel to me. You must kneel to God only and thank Him for your freedom. To

Negroes who knelt before him calling him the messiah, while Lincoln inspected Richmond, Virginia, after its fall, April 3, 1865.

* * *

No, leave it as a monument. When someone called: "Pull it down," as Lincoln momentarily gazed at Libby Prison in deserted Richmond.

* * *

I wonder if I could get a glass of water. After sitting in a chair in Jefferson Davis's deserted mansion in Richmond.

* * *

If I were in your place, I'd let 'em up easy, let 'em up easy. To General Godfrey Weitzel who asked how to treat the people conquered.

* * *

It has been intimated to me that the gentlemen who have acted as the legislature of Virginia, in support of the rebellion, may now desire to assemble at Richmond, and take measures to withdraw the Virginia troops, and other support from resistance to the General Government. If they attempt it, give them permission and protection, until, if at all, then attempt some action hostile to the United States, in which case you will notify them and give them reasonable time to leave; and at the end of which time, arrest any who may remain. To General Godfrey Weitzel, on April 6, 1865, offering, in a way, amnesty.

* * *

We shall sooner have the fame by hatching the egg than by smashing it. In reply to accusation of acting too slowly.

* * *

General Sheridan, when this peculiar war began, I thought a cavalryman should be six feet four high, but I've changed my mind—five feet four will do in a pinch.

* * *

I will tell you just what kind of a chap he is. He is one of those long-armed fellows with short legs that can scratch his shins without having to stoop over. When asked his opinion of General Philip H. Sheridan.

* * *

General Sheridan says "If the thing is pressed I think Lee will surrender." Let the thing be pressed. To General Grant on April 6, 1865.

* * *

Judge not, that ye be not judged. To Senator Charles Sumner and Mrs. Lincoln who were advocating that Jefferson Davis, when captured, be hanged.

* * *

I propose closing up this interview by the band performing a particular tune...I have always thought "Dixie" one of the best tunes I ever heard. To a huge crowd below the White House balcony, announcing the surrender of General General Robert E. Lee at 4:30 p.m. on April 9, 1865.

* * *

That was a pretty fair speech, I think, but you threw some light on it. To his friend Noah Brooks who held a candle while Lincoln addressed the crowd on April 11, 1865.

* * *

When I was a boy in Indiana, I went to a neighbor's house one morning and found a boy of my own size holding a coon on a string. I asked him what he had and what he was doing. He says, "It's a coon. Dad cotched six last night, and killed all but this poor little cuss. Dad told me to hold him until he came back, and I'm afraid he's going to kill this one too; and oh, Abe, I do wish he would get away!" "Well, why don't you let him loose?" "That wouldn't be right; and if I let him go, Dad would give me hell. But if he would get away himself, it would be all right." Now if Jeff Davis and those other fellows will only get away, it will be all right, but if we should catch them, and I should let them go, "Dad would give me hell." To friends in early April on what to do with Confederate leaders.

* * *

I know I am in danger; but I am not going to worry over threats like these. To William H. Seward, showing him the envelope marked "assassinations" which contained 80 items.

* * *

About ten days ago I retired very late. I had been up waiting for important dispatches from the front. I could not have been long in bed when I fell into a slumber, for I was weary. I soon began to dream. There seemed to be a death-like stillness about me. Then I heard subdued sobs as if a number of people were weeping. I thought I left my bed and wandered downstairs. There the silence was broken by the same pitiful sobbing, but the mourners were invisible. I went from room to room; no living person was in sight but the same mournful sounds of distress met me as I passed along. It was light in all the rooms; every object was familiar to me; but where were all the people who were grieving as if their hearts would break? I was puzzled and alarmed. What could be the meaning of all this? Determined to find the cause of a state of things so mysterious and so shocking, I kept on until I arrived at

the East Room, which I entered. There I met
with a sickening surprise. Before me was a
catafalque, on which rested a corpse wrapped
in funeral vestments. Around it were stationed
soldiers who were acting as guards; and there
was a throng of people, some gazing mourn-
fully upon the corpse, whose face was covered,
others weeping pitifully. "Who is dead in the
White House?" I demanded of one of the soldiers. "The President," was his answer. "He
was killed by an assassin!" Then came a loud
burst of grief from the crowd, which awoke
me from my dream. I slept no more that night;
and although it was only a dream I have been
strangely annoyed by it ever since. Reluctantly
giving an account of his dream to Chief of
Security Lamon and Mrs. Lincoln, the second
week in April.

* * *

Well, it's only a dream, Mary. Let us say
no more about it, and try to forget it. To his
wife who kept fretting about the dream.

* * *

To sleep; perchance to dream! Ay, there's the rub. To Chief of Security Lamon, quoting from *Hamlet*, in reference to the dream.

* * *

Hill, your apprehension of harm to me from some hidden enemy is downright foolishness. For a long time you have been trying to keep somebody—the Lord knows who—from killing me. Don't you see how it will turn out? In this dream it was not me, but some other fellow, that was killed. It seems that this ghostly assassin tried his hand on someone else. And this reminds me of an old farmer in Illinois whose family was made sick by eating greens. Some poisonous herb had got into the mess, and members of the family were in danger of dying. There was a half-witted boy in the family called Jake; and always afterward when they had greens the old man would say, "Now, afore we risk these greens, let's try 'em on Jake. If he stands 'em, we're all right." Just so with me. As long as this imaginary assassin continues to exercise himself on others I can stand it. Well, let it go. I think the Lord in His own good time and way will work this out all right. God knows what is best. To Ward H. Lamon, ending with a very deep sigh.

* * *

In the Civil War: lost in battle, from wounds or from disease, 620,000 Americans—360,000 from the North, and 260,000 from the South.

* * *

This talk about Mr. Davis tires me. I hope he will mount a fleet horse, reach the shores of the Gulf of Mexico, and ride so far into its waters that we shall never see him again. In response to those who wanted Jefferson Davis hanged from a sour apple tree.

* * *

It is a good face. I am glad the war is over at last. At the breakfast table, April 14, 1865, to his son Robert, home from the front and showing his father a picture of General Lee.

* * *

Creswell, you make me think of a lot of young folks who once started out Maying. To reach their destination they had to cross a shallow stream, and did so by means of an old flat boat. When they came to return, they found to their dismay that the old scow had disappeared. They were in sore trouble and thought over all manner of devices for getting over the water, but without avail. After a time one of the boys proposed that each fellow pick up the girl he liked the best and wade over with her. The masterly proposition was carried out until all that were left upon the island was a little short chap and a great, long, Gothic-built elderly lady. Now, Creswell, you are trying to leave me in the same predicament. You fellows are all getting your own friends out of this scrape, and you will succeed in carrying off one after another until nobody but Jeff Davis and myself will be left on the island, and then I won't know what to do. How should I feel? How should I look lugging him over? I guess the way to avoid such an embarrassing situation is to let them all out at once. To Senator John A. J. Creswell of Maryland asking for the release from prison of a rebel friend—toward noon, April 14, 1865.

* * *

I think it providential that this great rebellion is crushed just as Congress has adjourned and there are none of the disturbing elements of that body to hinder and embarrass us. If we are wise and discreet, we shall reanimate the States and get their governments in successful operations, with order prevailing and the Union reestablished before the Congress comes together in December...I hope there will be no persecution, no bloody work after the war is over. No one need expect me to take any part in hanging or killing those men, even the worst of them. Frighten them out of the country, open the gates, let down the bars, scare them off—enough lives have been sacrificed. To the cabinet with General Grant present—forenoon of April 14, 1865.

* * *

I had this strange dream again last night, and we shall, judging from the past, have great news very soon. I think it must be from Sherman. My thoughts are in that direction, as are most of yours. To the cabinet, referring to his previous odd and remarkable dreams before every great battle—April 14, 1865.

* * *

Well, I should not be sorry to have them out of the country; but I should be for following them up pretty close, to make sure of their going. An observation to the cabinet members about what to do with one hundred rebel leaders—April 14, 1865.

* * *

We can't undertake to run State governments in all these Southern States. Their people must do that—though I reckon that at first some of them may do it badly. To the cabinet on April 14, 1865, before adjourning for the next meeting on April 18.

After the cabinet meeting on April 14, Lincoln met privately with his vice president, Andrew Johnson from Tennessee.

* * *

There is time for all who need me. Let the good woman come in. To the guards who were trying to stop Nancy Bushrod, a black woman, from seeing the president.

* * *

My good woman, perhaps you will see many a day when all the food in the house is a single loaf of bread. Even so, give every child a slice and send your children off to school. To Nancy Bushrod who, with three children, was destitute because her husband had not received his army pay.

* * *

Well, no, I rather think not. When you have an elephant by the hind leg, and he's trying to run away, it's best to let him run. To Assistant Secretary of War Charles A. Dana, on whether to arrest a Confederate commissioner who engaged in anti-Union terrorism from Canada—April 14, 1865.

* * *

I never felt so happy in my life. To his wife, during an afternoon carriage ride with "just ourselves"—afternoon, April 14, 1865.

* * *

Crook, do you know, I believe there are men who want to take my life? And I have no doubt they will do it. To his guard as they were walking to the War Department late in the afternoon, passing some loud, drunken men— April 14, 1865.

* * *

I have perfect confidence in those who are around me—in every one of you men. I know no one could do it and escape alive. But if it is to be done, it is impossible to prevent it. To Crook, his guard, talking about the possibility of assassination—late afternoon, April 14, 1865.

* * *

That reminds me of the old story of the Scotch lassie on her way to market with a basket of eggs for sale. She had just forded a small stream with her skirts well drawn up when a wagoner on the opposite side of the stream called out, "Good morning, my lassie; how deep's the brook and what's the price of eggs?" She answered, "Knee deep and a sixpence!" To Charles A. Tinker, a telegraph operator, who explained difficult phrases to Lincoln.

* * *

It has been advertised that we will be there, and I cannot disappoint the people, otherwise I would not go. I do not want to go. To his guard Crook about going to the theater that night, April 14, 1865.

* * *

Good-bye, Crook. Not the usual, *Good-night, Crook!* Evening of April 14, 1865.

* * *

I am reminded of when I was a young man in Illinois, and a woman in the neighborhood made shirts. An Irishman went to her and ordered a white shirt for some special function. The woman made it, and laundered it and sent it to her customer. When he got it, the Irishman found the shirt had been starched all the way around, instead of only in the bosom, and he returned it with the remark that he didn't want a shirt that was all collar. The trouble with you, Shellabarger, is that you want the army all staff and no army. To Samuel Shellabarger who applied for a staff position for a constituent.

* * *

I survived the defeet uv Micklellan (who wuz, trooly, the nashen's hope and pride likewise), becoz I felt assoored that the rane uv the Goriller Linkin wood be a short wun; that in a few months, at furthest, Ginral Lee wood capcher Washington, depose the ape, and set up there a constooshnal guverment, based upon the great and immutable trooth that a white man is better than a nigger. (Instead) Lincoln rides into Richmond! An Illinois rale-splitter, a buffoon, an ape, a goriller, a smutty joker, set hisself down in President Davis's cheer, and rites dispatchis!...This ends the chapter. The Confederasy hez at last consentratid its last consentrate. It's ded. It's gathered up its feet, sed its last words, and deceest...Linkin will serve his term out—the tax on whisky won't be repeeled—our leaders will die off uv chagrin, and delirium tremens and inability to live so long out uv offis, and the sheep will be skattered. Farewell, vane world. Lincoln's reading from satirist Petroleum Vesuvius Nasby to Illinois Governor Dick Oglesby and Illinois Senator Dick Yates.

* * *

Why, if anyone else had been President and gone to Richmond, I would have been alarmed too; but I was not scared about myself a bit. To Speaker Schuyler Colfax who reminded him of the uneasiness of people about Lincoln's visit to a fallen Richmond.

* * *

April 14, 1865,
Allow Mr. Ashmun
& friend to come in
at 9:00 a.m. tomorrow
—A. Lincoln

Written on a card for Congressman George Ashmun of Massachusetts to get a cotton claim settled.

* * *

Grant thinks we can reduce the cost of the army establishment at least a half a million a day, which, with the reduction of expenditures of the navy, will soon bring down our national debt to something like decent proportions, and bring our national paper up to par, or nearly so, with gold—at least so they think. On his way to the carriage after leaving the White House for the Ford's Theater—evening, April 14, 1865.

* * *

Excuse me now, I am going to the theater. Come and see me in the morning. To Isaac N. Arnold of Chicago who asked Lincoln for a favor as he stepped into the carriage. These were the last words recorded of President Lincoln—as far as my research indicates—on Good Friday, April 14, 1865, about 8:45 p.m.